W9-ASJ-590

TWAYNE'S WORLD AUTHORS SERIES

A Survey of the World's Literature

Sylvia E. Bowman, Indiana University

GENERAL EDITOR

SPAIN

Gerald Wade, Vanderbilt University

EDITOR

Benito Pérez Galdós

TWAS 341

Benito Pérez Galdós

Benito Pérez Galdós

By WALTER T. PATTISON

Professor Emeritus
University of Minnesota

TWAYNE PUBLISHERS

A DIVISION OF G. K. HALL & CO., BOSTON

CARNEGIE LIBRARY
LIVINGSTONE COLLEGE
SALISBURY, N. C. 28144

Copyright © *1975 by G. K. Hall & Co.*
All Rights Reserved

Library of Congress Cataloging in Publication Data
Pattison, Walter Thomas, 1903-
    Benito Pérez Galdós.
    (Twayne's world author's series; TWAS 341: Spain)
    Bibliography: p. 173-77.
    Includes index.
    1. Pérez Galdós, Benito, 1843-1920.
PQ6555.Z5P28   863'.5   74-20650
ISBN 0-8057-2689-6

MANUFACTURED IN THE UNITED STATES OF AMERICA

863.5
P 438

Contents

96043

About the Author

Walter T. Pattison, Professor Emeritus of the University of Minnesota, was born in Chicago, January 5, 1903. He is the author of *Emilia Pardo Bazán* in the Twayne World Authors Series. His research interest was originally the Provençal troubadours; in later life he concentrated on Galdós. Among his publications are *The Life and Works of the Troubadour Raimbaut d'Orange, Benito Pérez Galdós and the Creative Process,* and *El naturalismo español.* He contributed a chapter on "Naturalism and the Spanish Novel" to *The Literature of the Western World* (London, Aldus Books) and articles to various learned journals, especially to the *Anales Galdosianos.*

While Pattison has spent most of his years as an active teacher at the University of Minnesota, he was also at Wesleyan University for ten years and served as a Visiting Professor at The University of Wisconsin, the University of California at Los Angeles, and the Universidad de San Carlos, Guatemala. Outside the intellectual field he enjoys outdoor sports — canoeing, fishing, and hunting.

Preface

Benito Pérez Galdós, universally considered as second only to Cervantes in the Spanish novel, is perhaps the least known author of comparable fame. Every cranny of the lives of Balzac, Dickens, and Tolstoy has been probed; yet unexplored gulfs remain in the biography of their reticent Spanish peer. As a result, myths about him circulate with the authority of fact. Even persons who knew him well were often misinformed. For example, Gregorio Marañón, Galdós's doctor in his old age, speaks incorrectly of the novelist's "English blood" (*Elogio y nostalgia de Toledo*, p. 153). Others erroneously say that he spoke English before he knew Spanish. Galdós himself is often inaccurate in dates he ascribes to events of his life; he even deliberately misleads us, as when he declares his novels were not planned in advance of writing.

As a consequence I have sought to verify with documentary sources as many of the events of Don Benito's life as possible. Fortunately the Casa-Museo Pérez Galdós in Las Palmas now has much of the author's private archives. In addition many letters to Galdós and a limited number of those from Galdós have been printed, clarifying many moot points in his life and facilitating the interpretation of his works.

The present writer has given especial attention to documents concerning Galdós's finances, a subject heretofore dismissed by many as unworthy of consideration when dealing with a literary genius. If I give prominence to money matters, it is because I see this as a central subject in Don Benito's life and as having had an important influence on his literary production.

It is my hope that this volume will appeal not only to the cultivated nonspecialist, for whom the Twayne Series is primarily intended, but that it will also stimulate Galdosian scholars to further researches toward the revelation of the real Galdós.

WALTER T. PATTISON

Marine on St. Croix
Minnesota

Chronology

1879   *sodes,* and writes the three-volume *Familia de León Roch* (Leon Roch's Family).

1880   He spends the winter of 1879 - 1880 and the following summer in Santander with his brother Ignacio and his family. He publishes nothing; reads Zola.

1881 - Galdós's period of mitigated naturalism which includes six
1885   novels, from *La desheredada* (The Disinherited Woman) to *Lo prohibido* (Forbidden Fruit).

1883   He makes his first trip to England; explores London.

1885   In January, Galdós receives a gift of *War and Peace* in French translation. In the summer, he travels through Portugal with Pereda.

1886   Galdós "elected" to the Congress as a Liberal. He writes, but does not publish, volume one of *Fortunata y Jacinta.* He takes a trip to the Rhineland.

1887   Benito's mother dies on April 12. He publishes the first two volumes of *Fortunata . . .* after having published almost nothing for two years. He travels to England and northern Europe with his friend José Alcalá Galiano.

1888   Visits the Exposition of Barcelona in May, where he dines with royalty. In the autumn he travels to Italy with Alcalá Galiano.

1889   Galdós is elected to the Royal Spanish Academy (June 13) after an initial defeat (January 19). He visits Edinburgh and Stratford upon Avon; goes to Paris, then to the Rhineland, where he joins Emilia Pardo Bazán.

1890   Galdós's term in Congress ends. He spends the winter in Santander, where he buys land for his house (San Quintín). Writes two volumes of *Angel Guerra.*

1891   Galdós's natural daughter María born in Santander on January 12.

1892   Premiere of *Realidad* (Reality), Galdós's first play to be performed, on March 15.

1894   His play *La de San Quintín* (*The Duchess of San Quintín*) produced on January 27; his first outstanding success in the theater. On October 13 his sister-in-law Magdalena dies in San Quintín. From October 16 to November 9 Galdós visits Las Palmas, where he receives a triumphal welcome. On December 11 his play *Los condenados* (The Condemned) fails.

1895   He writes the spiritually oriented novels *Nazarín* and *Halma.*

Chronology

1896 -   Galdós breaks off partnership with Miguel de la Cámara and
1898   sets up his own publishing house.
1897   He writes *Misericordia* (Compassion).
1898 -   He writes the Third Series of *National Episodes*.
1900
1901   On January 30 *Electra* is produced; it is a triumphal success,
         more political than literary.
1902 -   Galdós writes the Fourth Series of *National Episodes*.
1907
1905   He suffers a hemiplegic stroke.
1906   On July 25 his daughter María's mother, Lorenza Cobián,
         commits suicide. Galdós has first operation on his eyes.
1907   He is elected a Republican (i.e., anti-Monarchical) Repre-
         sentative for Madrid.
1907 -   He writes the six volumes of the incomplete Fifth Series of
1912   *National Episodes*.
1911   In May he undergoes an unsuccessful operation on his left
         eye for cataracts.
1912   In April his right eye is operated on without success. The
         campaign to get him the Nobel prize fails.
1914   He is elected a Republican Representative for Gran Canaria.
1915   He writes his last novel, *La razón de la sinrazón* (The Reason
         of Unreason).
1918   His last play, *Santa Juana de Castilla* (Saint Juana of Castile)
         produced.
1919   On January 19 his statue in the Retiro Park is unveiled.
1920   On January 4 Galdós dies. A multitude of common people
         pay homage to Galdós at his funeral the next day.

CHAPTER 1

A Very Private Person

I An Ambivalent Personality

NOT infrequently biographers look at the parents of their subjects to try to discover inherited traits or formative pressures that explain the personality of the biographees. In the case of Benito Pérez Galdós, very little ascendancy can be attributed to his father, Sebastián Pérez, and thus the predominant influence must be ascribed to his mother, the daughter of a Basque transferred to the Canary Islands.

From his mother, Dolores Galdós, Don Benito inherited certain characteristics of the Basques, most easily observed in his physical appearance. Like the Basques he "was tall and somewhat rough-hewn in body and features, as if carved of stone; . . . his eyes were small and timid, his face not very expressive, his manner of speaking brief, fragmentary, and low-pitched; in short, he did not give, even to those most enthusiastic about his work, that impression of genius which we imagine in great men."[1] His was the body of an athlete clothing a shy, withdrawing spirit. A man who preferred to listen rather than talk; one who suffered the keenest stage fright about speaking in public; yet one who, on the printed page, could fight valiantly for his ideals.

His public image and his true personality were poles apart, simply because he could never give free play to his real self except among his intimates. "Because in the depth of his soul, Galdós is a timid man. He has renown, health and strength, but he lacks that self-assuredness of attitude which so many others, far less worthy, exhibit everywhere. He feels rather embarrassed in public."[2] He avoided solemn and official occasions; refused invitations to dine in aristocratic company; even hated the frock coat which was the proper garb for such gatherings.[3]

As a consequence of this timidity, people who sought him out regularly came away disillusioned. Dr. Gregorio Marañón, his close friend, often introduced strangers to him, and he always warned them that "He is a man just like all the rest." "His simplicity was so great that at times it bordered on commonness."[4] This is the public Galdós that the young writers of the early twentieth century often compared to a grocer ("Don Benito el garbancero").

After Galdós became a dramatist his awkward, frightened appearance at curtain calls heightened the contrast between the genius and the timid, ordinary man. Berkowitz describes his first curtain call as follows: "For the vast majority of the spectators this was their first opportunity to see Galdós in person. He was a somewhat painful sight. Literally shoved out from behind the scenes, he came to an awkward, rigid halt in front of the footlights, the personification of fright and terror!"[5] It was easy to conclude that the trembling, pathetic figure on the stage was not a genius at all, and that only an exaggerated evaluation of his own importance had brought him before the public.

So much for the image Galdós the man (not his writings) produced in those who saw him only superficially. We turn now to his hidden, real person, revealed only in private and to people with whom he sympathized.

Manuel Ugarte's first impression of Galdós was very different from what the spectators had seen in the theater. "He received me with that openness [characteristic] of those who know their own worth and don't need to improvise a superiority with vain protocolary formulas. Nothing more simple and affectionate than his handshake. And nothing more simple than his conversation, which gradually became familiar until it ended as chatting with a friend. . . . His words tended to make one forget the literary man. He was a companion who gave opinions and asked questions ingenuously without worrying about the effect which they could produce."[6] How different from the Galdós of the curtain calls! His simplicity and straightforwardness have become virtues.

Because most people did not know the real Galdós legends grew up around him. Everyone knew that he produced many novels; consequently it was assumed that writing was his only and constant activity, precluding all other interests. He was said to have practically no friends. His relations with other members of his family were unknown and of course overlooked. The notion that he had innumerable fleeting love affairs became widespread. Since Galdós himself did nothing to destroy these myths, it seemed to many that he accepted them as true. It pained him to talk about his personal

life, and rather than deny a falsehood by a frank disclosure of his
private existence, he preferred to let the erroneous notion flourish.

The last ten years have seen the publication of numerous letters to
Galdós and a small portion of those which Don Benito wrote to
friends and acquaintances. Here at last we can peek behind the curtain of privacy which guarded him from impertinent eyes.
Specifically, what do we learn about the statement that Galdós had
very few friends? To mention only those regarded as especially good
friends would be to name at least thirty or forty persons. Wherever
his activities took him he formed cordial and enduring relationships.

By no means all of his friends have left a historical trace, as very
many of them were not of exalted status. "In Toledo Galdós had
numerous friends, almost always of that social stratum on the limit
between the proletariat and the middle class, in which he especially
liked to live."[7] Later, when he already enjoyed a great literary
reputation, he sought out in Las Palmas a boyhood crony, Joaquín
Gutiérrez, a "carpenter, tinsmith, talker, and drinker,"[8] and spent a
couple of hours every day with him. Most of the Canary Islanders
residing in Madrid with whom the youthful Galdós passed the time
in the Café Universal, as well as those that gathered daily in the
mature author's publishing house, were of the middle class and unknown to fame.

Letters such as those exchanged between Dr. Tolosa Latour and
the novelist[9] sparkle with witticisms. The two men call each other by
nicknames and banter and jest in a playful tone. Don Benito, contrary to the myth, was really an entertaining and delightful conver-
sationalist with his intimates. With children, too, he let himself go
and overcame "his incurable timidity" which he showed to people
who were not his familiars. "But with children . . . he unbosomed
himself in an abundant and gay torrent of words, full of clever
childish sayings, mixed with the experience, full of humor, of his vast
and profound life."[10]

II *Family Obligations and Charity*

It has always been known that Galdós lived with one or two of his
sisters, a nephew, and a sister-in-law. It seems that most biographers
feel that these relatives were doing Don Benito a favor — they were
keeping house for him, looking after his practical affairs, even helping him by copying his manuscripts.[11] Such an interpretation of the
domestic situation accords with the myth of the withdrawn author
concerned only with the rapid, mechanical production of novels.

The letters now available tell a different tale. Galdós had to take on the position of head of the family, after the death of his parents and his oldest brother. Although he was the youngest of the ten children, his financial success as an author caused him to assume family debts, which ultimately contributed to his impoverished old age. Even his household, sheltering a number of his relatives, represented a considerable expense.

It would be incorrect to think of this family aid as given grudgingly. The letters show Galdós sincerely worried over the health of his little niece Micaela, using all of his prestige to gain an appointment for his brother Ignacio, indignant when an attempt is made to force his nephew José Hurtado de Mendoza out of his job.[12] We can only conclude that he was very much of a family man, quietly but deeply involved.

This man, whose affective life was a closed book to most of his contemporaries, was charitable and kind. His friend Pereda claimed that "he was very profuse with his possessions, particularly with the needy; and his heart and the door of his house were always open to other people's wants."[13] He loved not only children, as we have seen, but plants and animals. When he built himself a house in Santander he had earth moved into the rocky terrain to establish a garden and plant trees. The love of trees was almost a religion in Galdós's house. He kept records of the number of tomatoes he gathered and the yield of eggs from his chickens. Not infrequently photographs show him with one of his canine friends. He once saved a black lamb destined for slaughter because of its color, and kept it as a pet in his Madrid home. This animal followed him like a dog and even when returned to the farm always recognized its master when he came to visit.[14]

III *Religion*

A profound love of nature connotes a spiritual or even religious orientation. Certainly this is true in the present case. But Don Benito's spirit could not be encompassed in the narrow dogmatic Catholicism which had a wide acceptance in nineteenth-century Spain. This reactionary doctrine, known as *neocatolicismo* ("Neo-Catholicism"), sought to curb freedom of thought by censorship of the press and of university lectures; it combated any attempt to introduce into Spain any other faith than the state-supported Catholic church; it extolled the Inquisition and would have gladly seen a return to force used to impose Catholicism. In politics Neo-Catholicism supported the Absolutist Pretender, Don Carlos, and hoped, by means of civil war, to place him on the throne. Galdós's stern, puritanical mother was in sympathy with Neo-Catholicism although probably not concerned with its political program.

The object of the wrath of the Neo-Catholics were the Liberals, in which category Galdós found his spiritual home. Liberalism was a broad term, including a spectrum of opinion stretching from atheism to an unexaggerated, tolerant Catholicism. The Liberals were united more by opposition to, and at times persecution by, the Neo-Catholics than by a consistency of their own beliefs. But they did share an attitude of tolerance — a willingness to concede that other philosophies and other religions contained some good. They also all recognized the validity of free thought: that is, they believed that men had the right to examine logically and to accept or reject any idea, even if it were a religious dogma.

When Galdós came to Madrid as a student at the age of nineteen, a liberal philosophy had taken hold among some professors and students. Called Krausism after a minor German philosopher, its appeal to Spaniards was undoubtedly due first, to its insistence on tolerance, and secondly, to its application of ethics to everyday life. The Krausists thought that men should live nobly and simply, dedicating their lives to the service and enlightenment of their fellows in contrast to the Neo-Catholics' concern with ritual to the neglect of private morals.

Galdós studied history under Fernando de Castro, a Krausist whom he praised in one of his journalistic articles, and he became a good friend of other members of the Krausist group, notably Francisco Giner de los Ríos, whose saintly life represented the flowering of the principles of the new philosophy. Krausism, we shall see, is an important element in some of Galdós's novels. Its spirit was to stay with him all of his life.

Against this background of religious and philosophic beliefs, we can see in Don Benito both a negative and a positive religious phase. He can and does write many journalistic articles against the Neo-Catholics and he can attack their outworn beliefs vigorously in some of his novels. But in other works he can show his love for a priest who sincerely tries to live by the example of Jesus, or he can extol the pure charity of a serving maid who begs in the streets to support her impoverished employer. He can write a drama (*Electra*) which became a veritable rallying cry of the anticlerical forces and which brought him letters urging compliance with the official church or even threatening his life:[15] but he can be described by one who knew him intimately as "not only a man fundamentally good, but also profoundly religious." Dr. Marañón goes on to say that he would like to write Galdós's biography specifically in order to "destroy the legend of his skepticism and to show the profound mysticism of his refined soul," which latter is laid bare in his novel *Angel Guerra*. In the cathedral of Toledo Galdós, like Angel, allowed his "buried, but living, religion" to surface and he listened to the services with deep spiritual participation.[16] Like Angel, Don Benito loved to visit the many out-of-the-way convents of Toledo, to attend their early morning offices, and to exchange a few words with the soft-spoken nuns.

IV *Tolerance*

Menéndez y Pelayo, who in one of his early writings could accuse Galdós of being "the implacable and cold enemy of Catholicism,"[17] in later life says that Don Benito "has never been a skeptic nor a frivolous spirit. Religion would not intervene so frequently in his novels, if he himself did not feel an aspiration to religion more or less defined and concrete, but [in any case] undeniable."[18]

In short, Galdós was a bitter enemy of clericalism, that is, of the intrusion of priests into politics, education, and other areas that the laity considered its province. He especially detested the idea of a single state religion and acclaimed freedom of conscience, the freedom to choose whatever religion gave spiritual satisfaction.[19]

Contrasting his religious doubts with his friend Pereda's unquestioning faith Don Benito says: "He is a serene spirit, I a perturbed, restless spirit. He knows where he is going, he starts from a fixed base. Those of us who doubt what he affirms are seeking the truth, and we run constantly toward the place where we think we see it, beautiful and elusive."[20] He is not the implacable enemy of Catholicism. He writes: "Catholicism is the most perfect of established religions, but no established religion, not even Catholicism, satisfies the thought or the *heart* of the individual of our days. Nobody can eradicate this idea from me . . . Doubt about certain things is so rooted in me that nothing can eliminate it."[21] Very much the typical modern man, he yearned for and sought, rather than possessed, final truth.

One of the strong positive traits of Galdós's character was his tolerance, even of those whose opinions conflicted with his own. We have just seen him speaking of, and writing to, Pereda, an archconservative but still an intimate friend. José María de Pereda disliked all things modern. For him village life was the ideal. In politics and religion he was an unshakable reactionary.

The flowering of these relations with conservatives came when Don Benito entered the Royal Academy, sponsored by Menéndez y Pelayo; in his turn, a few days later, Galdós served Pereda in a like capacity. We should note that it was Don Benito's tolerance, not that of Pereda, that kept this friendship alive. "Our pleasant conversations often ended in disputes, whose intensity never passed the limits of cordiality. Many times, moved by my conciliatory nature, I yielded in my opinions. Pereda never yielded. He is irreducible, monolithic . . . He conquered in me relatively vast zones more easily than I inches of territory in him."[22] So Galdós, certainly most intolerant of Neo-Catholicism, was tolerance itself with the leading Neo-Catholic writer.

V *Women*

One of the most persistent myths about Galdós is that he had a "pathological" interest in sex. He is reputed to have had numerous furtive affairs, about which he was never willing to talk, and which are supposed to have contributed substantially to his poverty in his old age.[23] No one can deny that he did have affairs, but the exaggeration of this aspect of his life is considerable. He had a brief affair with Emilia Pardo Bazán.[24] He did have an illegitimate daughter, María, about whom we shall write later. But no record of earlier love affairs remains. After 1900, when Don Benito's health and personality were progressively disintegrating he had a close friendship with "a cultured and refined old lady of moderate wealth, named Teodosia Gandarias."[25] This relationship lasted up to the year of Galdós's death. The lonely old author had become blind; he was ignored or even disdained by most of the younger literary men; his sisters Concepción and Carmen and his well-loved sister-in-law were dead. This explains why he valued so highly Teodosia's warm admiration. People who knew him in his senile, impoverished old age extrapolated his interest in Teodosia back to his early years and assumed that he always had this same interest in women. But Galdós himself — perhaps an unreliable witness — attributed his good health to his methodical life and to the fact he hadn't "led a depraved life."[26] Even in his last years "he spoke with great respect of women, and admired especially those who were self-sufficient. On one occasion he said to me 'The day when women succeed in emancipating themselves, the world will be different.' He always liked active, energetic, industrious women."[27] No doubt there were some amorous entanglements with women of the lower classes,[28] but if Galdós, as some claim, was so promiscuous, why were his sisters so devoted to him? Such excess could hardly be regarded as honorable. Berkowitz implies that he had various illegitimate children.[29] We may ask why Don Benito, known to have been a great lover of children and who treats children with sympathetic tenderness in his writings, did not recognize *all* these supposed offspring, instead of limiting himself to just one.

We may also ask why Galdós did not marry, especially since he spent the winter of 1890 - 91 in Santander (where María was born on January 12, 1891),[30] which reveals his affection for, and feeling of responsibility toward, María's mother, Lorenza Cobián. But she was of a humble social class, the daughter of peasants, and besides a wife would have meant the breaking off of his regular established habits and the probable abandonment of his sisters and nephew. The inertia of resistance to change may have been the deciding factor. It is also probable that the marriages he had observed were not very happy and made him suspicious of the relationship. There are relatively few successful marriages in his novels. Galdós's first novel, *La sombra* (The Apparition) revolves around marital jealousy which drives the husband insane. The author makes it clear that infidelity and suspicion of infidelity have ruined marriages from the earliest beginnings of the institution.[31] Is he simply using his artistic imagination to put appropriate words in the mouth of one of his characters or are his ideas on marriage visible in this attitude?

The happy, elderly name-character of *Pedro Minio* (1908) has an "ideal friendship" with an old woman which reminds us of Galdós's dedication to Teodosia, and perhaps Pedro's boasting about the many conquests of his younger days refers to supposed love affairs of the author himself. But Sister Bonifacia, head of the asylum where Pedro lives, calls his stories of courting "atrociously fantastic" (act 2, scene 6). There is no question about Galdós's liking women, but must it be assumed that all his relationships with them were carnal?[32]

There is a strong possibility that a desire for liberty lay behind Don Benito's rejection of the bonds of matrimony. Free love is the ideal of a number of his characters, including women — Augusta in *Realidad* and Tristana in the novel which bears her name. Don Evaristo Feijoo, in *Fortunata y Jacinta*, is the philosopher of free love, taking a position halfway between *natural* love, without social control, and the institutionalized love of marriage. Certainly Galdós sympathizes with these characters who may indeed express his own opinion.[33] Free love, as he conceived it, is not to be compared with licentiousness. It is rather the freedom of each partner to develop fully his own personality and his own creativity. It was a relationship into which our timid author never entered (unless we consider his "ideal friendship" with Teodosia to be such a one) but of which he no doubt dreamed.

In conclusion, we see Galdós as a very timid man, expansive only with children and close friends. A great observer of all he saw and heard, he seldom needed to take notes but depended on his powerful memory. Imagination was a strong element in his makeup, but throughout his early years he systematically distrusted it and often shows excessive imagination as the cause of his fictional characters' misfortunes. He admits that he is a stubborn man; this trait made it possible for him to produce regularly and abundantly, rising early and writing five or six hours every morning. Very charitable, very simple in his tastes in food and clothes, religious in his own way, endowed with a quiet sense of humor, he was a man often misunderstood by his contemporaries.

CHAPTER 2

From Las Palmas to Madrid

I *The Galdós Family*

IN 1823 Sebastián Pérez married María de los Dolores Galdós. Twenty years later (May 10, 1843) the last of their ten children, the future novelist, Benito, was born. Everyone agrees that Doña Dolores was the dominant partner in her marriage and that her strong will, her rigid puritanical religiosity, and her love of a well-ordered routine made her a despot within her home. She came by these traits from her father, Domingo Galdós, who was a Basque, born in Azpeitia, also the birthplace of Saint Ignatius of Loyola. Domingo became a secretary of the Inquisition and was assigned to a post in Las Palmas in the Canary Islands. He had not taken holy orders and thus could marry a lady who figures in the family history more as the mother of eleven children than as a strong personality. On the other hand, Don Domingo is said to have "ruled his household with the austere dignity of his inquisitorial office,"[1] much in the way his daughter Dolores was to hold absolute sway over her family.

Her son Benito was to model some of his female characters on Doña Dolores, emphasizing their intolerant and dominating nature. The most notable example is Doña Perfecta (in the novel of the same name), a woman capable of ordering the murder of her nephew whose liberal ideas clashed with her traditionalism.[2] Although in Doña Perfecta Galdós undoubtedly exaggerated Dolores's traits for dramatic effect, we must conclude that he had no sympathy for his mother's life style. Yet there are ways in which his mother's heritage shows up in Benito: his Basque physique, his stubborn will, and his adherence to a well-ordered routine.

Dolores had a clannish sense of family solidarity. Even in the choice of a husband she made family matters paramount. Her father had died in poverty, so she insisted that her widowed mother live with the newlyweds from the very day of their marriage! Don Sebastián, sixteen years older than his wife, was modest and irresolute in his relations with her. With his children he seemed more a grandfather than a father. He had had his moments of glory, when he served as a lieutenant in the campaigns against the French in the Peninsular War. He loved to tell young Benito about these military exploits and the latter incorporated memories of his father's tales into his historical novels *(Episodios Nacionales)* which dealt with the same events. After the war Don Sebastián received a grant of land as a reward, and he also held the honorific title of Governor of the King's Castle.³ With the properties he inherited from his parents he was able to maintain decorously his large family in the house (Calle del Cano, Las Palmas) which is today the Pérez Galdós Museum.

Don Sebastián's house on the Calle del Cano was small for a family of four boys and six girls.⁴ We can understand better and sympathize more with Doña Dolores and her desire for order and discipline when we contemplate her crowded household. Of the girls, only the oldest, Carmen, married. When they were growing up she and her sister Concepción cared for and mothered their baby brother Benito. Concepción was to live with Benito in Madrid and Santander for many years until her death in 1914; Carmen spent her last years with Benito, and her two sons José and Hermenegildo were constantly protected and aided by the author.

II *Benito's Childhood and Youth*

Benito, despite his robust constitution during his middle years, was not a vigorous child. He impressed his playmates as a timid, inhibited youngster. He himself says "My temperament was always very nervous."⁵ But he states that he was "precocious" and that he learned to read at an early age. He showed considerable ability in drawing and modeling; later he painted well enough to win a prize in a Provincial Exposition.⁶ He continued painting in his mature years, especially during his vacations in Santander.⁷ The preserved youthful drawings are mostly caricatures of local politicians and the artists who were to perform in the new theater, which was built close to the shore of the ocean. Benito's sketches show operatic singers wearing life preservers and fish invading the auditorium. They reveal a sense of humor and a caustic realism.

Music also became important to him and continued to interest him throughout his life. His sister Dolores played the piano well and taught him the art. Later, in his first years in Madrid, he was an assiduous operagoer. Many of his early journalistic articles are critiques of operatic performances. Both he and his nephew José were pianists; after Galdós learned to play the organ they combined their talents to render versions of symphonic works. One of his friends says that Don Benito knew all Beethoven's works by heart;[8] the author himself tells us that he used Beethoven's music as the framework of a play, *Alma y vida* (1902).[9]

While these extracurricular artistic interests were developing Benito revealed very little of the same spirit in school. His music teacher in the Colegio de San Agustín could not even remember that the future novelist had been one of his students.[10] His report card shows him earning good grades,[11] but he seemed an absent-minded, uninterested youth. Yet even during school study periods he was beginning to write.

Some of his essays and one satirical poem were published in a local newspaper.[12] Other schoolboy writings — some assigned and others confiscated by his teachers — found their way into the city library.[13] These juvenalia add nothing to the author's reputation but they do show traits which were to predominate in his later work: an inclination toward realism rather than fantasy and close observation of his social environment.

Benito finished his secondary education in 1862. He had been talking about studying architecture while Doña Dolores was insisting on his becoming a lawyer. There seems to have been more than one reason why she wanted him at the law school in Madrid. She not only regarded the legal profession as a most exalted one; she also wanted to remove Benito from influences she considered pernicious.

Domingo Pérez Galdós, Benito's oldest brother, had married Magdalena Hurtado de Mendoza y Tate, and the latter's brother, José Hermenegildo, married Carmen, Benito's favorite sister. The mother of these two new members of the family was Mary Adriana Tate, born in Charleston, South Carolina, in 1802, the daughter of a well-to-do sea captain who traded frequently with Cuban ports, including Trinidad de Cuba, where Adriana lived after her marriage. At least one of the Galdós family, José María, also lived there. When Adriana's husband died, she entered into an irregular union with José María (Benito's uncle) and gave birth to a daughter, Sisita. This girl was about two or three years younger than Benito and her mother brought her to Las Palmas in 1850, at which time Domingo and Magdalena built an elegant house in the city.

Doña Dolores had not approved of the free and easy manners of Magdalena and José Hermenegildo; now she was brought face to face with a scandal bringing shame on the family. Her consternation increased as she saw that Benito enjoyed the company of Adriana, and it reached its peak when it became evident that he was strongly attracted to Sisita. A separation of the two young people seemed imperative. So Benito went to Tenerife to be examined for the *bachillerato* ("secondary-school degree") and without returning to Las Palmas, embarked for Cádiz in September, 1862.

III *First Years in Madrid*

The mainland was like a foreign country to him. From Cádiz — his first large city — he took his first train, that nineteenth-century symbol of progress, as far as Córdoba, where the rails ended and the traveler changed to a stagecoach. Spain was a mixture of the old and the new, something which was true even of the capital city, the center of all new and progressive elements and yet the residence of a growing population of newly arrived peasants, almost all illiterate. The city fell into two clearly differentiated parts: the *barrios bajos* ("low districts") to the south, teeming, animated, and popular; the bourgeois and aristocratic area to the north, where the tall silk hat and frock coat proclaimed the serious respectability and economic status of the male inhabitants. It was a fascinating place to explore. During the next decade, Benito spent much time wandering through the streets, acquiring an unsurpassed knowledge of the city, which was to be the scene of most of his novels. He read the essayists who wrote of Madrilenian customs. He especially delighted in the playlets, most depicting life in the low quarters, written by the late eighteenth-century author, Ramón de la Cruz. Reminiscences of, and even quotations from, these little farces appear in many of Galdós's historical novels.[14] He even dreamed that Don Ramón accompanied him on his tours of the popular district.[15]

In theory, Benito's purpose in Madrid was the study of law. In those days there was a year of preliminary studies before tackling legal materials. The curriculum of the first year included history, taught by the defrocked priest, Fernando de Castro, for whom Galdós had great respect. He refers to him as a wise professor "whom young people reverence and admire."[16] He also studied Latin literature with Alfredo Adolfo Camús, whose witty lectures entranced the students. Camús adored "classical Greek beauty" and abhorred "all conventionality." An enemy of crude realism, he attacked modern French literature and its influence on music and the plastic arts. He upheld as models the Greeks, Shakespeare, Cervantes, and Erasmus.[17] Benito also admired his professor of Greek, Lázaro Bardón, about whom he wrote another laudatory essay.[18]

After this first year Galdós's record at the university was very poor. He scraped through the program of 1863 - 64 with low grades but afterward failed every year because of nonattendance of classes. Still he continued to register at the university up to 1867 - 68 since it was his excuse for being in Madrid. What was Benito doing with his time?

As we shall see, he was giving much of it to writing, but he was also educating himself. The fruitful readings during this period were extensive and widely varied.[19] The focus of his intellectual life was the Atheneum, a literary and artistic club which sponsored lectures and discussion groups and had a good library. Referring to the old location of the Atheneum in the Calle de la Montera, Galdós speaks of "the old Atheneum, which is my Atheneum, my literary cradle, the fertile atmosphere where the poor flowers that youthful ambition sowed in my heart germinated and grew."[20]

Why could Benito give so much credit to the Atheneum? A glance at its various programs during his early years in Madrid shows us the range of lectures and discussions he could have, and probably did, attend.[21] The forum was open to the most diverse opinions. While the liberal ideas of the Krausists were predominant, the opponents of the philosophy also held forth. Academic freedom, the right of the professor to teach what he believes without censorship, was both attacked and defended. The possibility of a union of Spain and Portugal, the relations of church and state, and those of capital and labor were all topics of discussions. Subjects which have direct relevance to some of Galdós's works were the compatibility or incompatibility of Catholicism and freedom, the history of the Spanish Jews, the political history of Spain from 1820 to 1823, and various lectures on the philosophy and methodology of history. Literature was well represented: Camús gave a series of lectures on Renaissance humanists; Valera, who had just produced his famous novel *Pepita Jiménez*, talked on the literature of the nineteenth century; German literature was covered in two separate series; and a discussion group took idealism versus realism as its theme. Galdós was above all a listener; yet perhaps his inactivity has been too greatly exaggerated. On December 27, 1872, he was elected vice president of the section of literature, of which Juan Valera became the president and José

Alcalá Galiano, one of Benito's very close friends, a secretary.[22] In the informal, friendly atmosphere of the Atheneum it was easy to enter conversations and make friendships. Our shy author was drawn into relationships with men who became ardent champions of his work: Emilio Huelin, a mining engineer, and the youthful Armando Palacio Valdés and Leopoldo Alas (Clarín), both of whom were unconditionally devoted to Don Benito.

Although the Atheneum was, as we have seen, open to men of all opinions, the dominant tone was one of progressive, modern thought. The Krausists used it as a podium for popularizing their ideas. Galdós declares that "the Atheneum was for the revolution [of 1868] what the Encyclopedia was for the French Revolution"[23] and that "in that den,[24] for I must so call it, the Good News was born, and there it had its laborious gestation, until it gave to the Hispanic world the blessed fruit of democracy, laicism, minimum tolerance, the certain anticipation of greater conquests for the near future."[25] Don Benito underestimated the traditionalistic forces which were to cancel the influence of the liberal spirit but he correctly evaluated the role of the Atheneum in propagating a spiritual renaissance.

IV *Student Life*

During these early years Benito lived in various boarding houses, most of whose inhabitants were students given to boisterous pranks as well as serious discussions. His novel *El Doctor Centeno* gives us a picture of this life that is undoubtedly based on personal recollections. Of course the young men discussed recent plays, such as García Gutiérrez's *Venganza catalana* (Catalan Vengeance, 1864). Benito thrilled to this performance and dreamt of attaining instant fame by writing a drama.[26] He tried his hand at an historical play, *La expulsión de los moriscos* (The Expulsion of the Moors), and a comedy of manners, *Un joven de provecho* (A Useful Young Man), neither one of which was produced or published during his lifetime. His other early plays have been destroyed.

The students also had their share in demonstrations against the government of Queen Isabel II. When she forced the resignation of Emilio Castelar (at that time a university professor, later to become a president of the first Spanish republic) as well as that of the rector of the university, the students replied with a manifestation violently repressed by the armed forces. Benito received saber blows on his back, nothing of importance in a riot which saw many severely wounded or killed.

A year after the affair just mentioned an abortive revolution (June 22, 1866) ended with the arrest and execution of the sergeants of the St. Gil barracks. Benito witnessed the file of coaches taking the sergeants to their death, and he calls it "the most tragic, sinister spectacle that I have ever seen." He adds: "Overcome with grief, along with my friends, I saw them pass. I didn't have valor enough to follow the funeral cortege to the place of execution, and I ran to my house to seek alleviation of my pain in my beloved books and in imaginary dramas which are more entertaining than real ones."[27] In his novel *Angel Guerra* Galdós makes his hero witness the execution and suffer from nightmares in which circumstances of the tragic scene haunt him. Clearly the events of the uprising of the sergeants compounded Benito's feelings inspired by the earlier repression of the students.

Boarding house life was extended beyond the limits of the house itself into the cafés. The same mixture of banter and seriousness prevailed around the coffee table. Galdós gives us a long disquisition on cafés and the peculiarities of the habitués in *Fortunata y Jacinta*, where discussions of politics, economics, and of spiritualism alternate with joking.[28] Of course, Benito had observed many similar episodes in various cafés. His favorite coffee house was the Café Universal, located on the Puerta del Sol, the gathering place of the Canary Islanders in Madrid.

V *Early Travels*

Travel soon became another educative force in Galdós's development. He returned to Las Palmas in the summers of 1863, 1864, and 1869, after which he visited his birthplace only in 1894. Unsympathetic critics tend to reprove what they call his indifference to his native land. It is possible that his lingering affection for Sisita had much to do with his first two visits; later, when she had returned to Cuba, married, and died, it is conceivable that a feeling of sadness became associated with his memories of home. Furthermore, his widowed sister-in-law Magdalena established herself in Madrid about 1870 and allowed her antagonism toward Benito's mother to prevail. She and her husband had helped the young author financially in the publication of his first novel and had taken him on his second trip to France, and she demanded obedience in return. A point on which she insisted was his severance of relations with the island.[29]

In 1867 Magdalena's brother José Hermenegildo Hurtado de

Mendoza took his young son José and Benito to Paris, where an International Exposition was in progress. "Devoured by a feverish curiosity I passed the whole day going up and down the streets, my city map in hand, admiring its many monuments, mingling with the cosmopolitan crowd which churned about everywhere. In a week of this activity I already knew Paris as if it were a Madrid ten times larger. I made frequent stops at the book stalls . . . along the Seine. The first book I bought was a little volume of Balzac's works. . . ."[30] Although Don Benito says this was his introduction to the French novelist, he mentions one of Balzac's characters in *La sombra* (The Apparition) possibly written the year before this trip. In any case he soon completed his collection of eighty volumes of Balzac and he refers to him in flattering terms in a journalistic article written in 1868.[31]

Galdós did not enjoy the International Exposition. "If I am to tell the truth, the exposition made me dizzy, befuddled me, and I always came out of it with a headache. I enjoyed admiring the artistic jewels of the Louvre and the Luxembourg or the archaeological treasures of the Cluny Museum. But my greatest joy was to witness the grand public ceremonies, like the military parade when the emperor [Napoleon III] reviewed the troops in the Champs Élysées."[32] He also saw the parades accompanying the entrance of foreign monarchs: the King of Portugal, the Sultan of Turkey, and King William of Prussia, who was to defeat Napoleon III three years later.

The next summer (1868) Benito returned to France with Domingo and Magdalena. This time they visited other parts of the country, not just Paris. He mentions Orleans, Bagnères de Bigorre, and Cauterets in the Pyrenees, and he tells us that he was writing his first published novel, *La fontana de oro* (The Golden Fountain), while on this trip. Afterward they journeyed to Provence, stopping at Avignon and Marseilles, and returned to Spain via Montpellier and Perpignan. Once in Spain Benito was able to acquaint himself thoroughly with Gerona, a city which was to be the scene of one of his *National Episodes,* although at the time he had no intention of writing this historical novel.

After Gerona the travelers proceeded to Barcelona, where they were greeted by news of the uprising against Isabel II, afterward known as "the glorious revolution" or "the Revolution of September." Benito's fellow travelers, frightened by the political upheaval, insisted on their all embarking on a ship leaving for the Canaries; but when the vessel reached Alicante the novelist disembarked and returned to Madrid. He reached the city just in time to see the entrance of the victorious General Serrano and the explosion of popular enthusiasm for the change of government.[33]

Throughout this decade, 1862 - 1873, Benito was writing. We have mentioned his futile efforts to win fame as a dramatist and his early novels. The bulk of his writing, however, was in journalism, to which we now turn our attention.

CHAPTER 3

Journalism and First Novels

I *Journalism*

WE know that Benito had already contributed to periodicals of Las Palmas, hence it is not surprising that his interest in journalism continued after his arrival in Madrid. He worked for several newspapers and magazines, most of which had a common orientation toward political liberalism and progressive reform. Although his articles were usually not on political themes, Galdós does make frequent attacks on the reactionary *neo-católicos* and often advocates municipal improvements; thus he aligns himself with the spirit of the *progresista* newspapers, which were promoting a revolution against Queen Isabel II. These papers proclaimed themselves "progressive" and "liberal," that is, in favor of constitutional government, universal suffrage, freedom of religious choice, and of free, compulsory primary schools.[1] In short, they wished to do away with the existing regime and to modernize Spain.

The men associated with Galdós on these periodicals were of course of this liberal persuasion. A number of them became his close friends. For example, the novelist praises José Ferreras as the kind of man Spain needs "for its moral and material progress." (*O.C.*, VI, 1515) Another example is José Luis Albareda, the owner of periodicals on which Don Benito worked and for two of which he was the chief editor. Albareda was prominent in politics as well as journalism. He believed in constitutional monarchy, rather like the English system, and consequently he opposed the rule of personal caprice characteristic of the Spanish Bourbons. He was wholly in favor of religious freedom of choice, condemning the idea of an imposed state religion and advocating a great reduction of the power of the clergy in governmental affairs.[2] Obviously he chose Galdós as the director of two of his periodicals because of the similarity of their beliefs.

The first major block of Galdós's journalistic work appears in *La Nación*, whose masthead carries the self-description "Diario Progresista" (Progressive Daily). Benito's first signed article is in the issue of February 3, 1865, and one hundred thirty-one signed or easily identified unsigned contributions of his were published during the next four years.[3] A number of them are verbal portraits of literary men or political figures; many others are weekly reviews of current events. There is also literary criticism of theatrical productions, critiques of operatic performances, and an occasional article on expositions of painting. One important contribution is devoted to Charles Dickens. It appears in the same number (March 9, 1868) containing the first installment of Galdós's translation of *Pickwick Papers*.

El Debate, a paper founded by Albareda and General Prim to support the new king Amadeo de Saboya, was directed by Don Benito. Speaking of *El Debate*, Galdós stated in 1912 that "its columns are full of my work. I wrote innumerable articles on politics, literature, art, and criticism."[4] If so, almost all of his work is unsigned. The paper does publish, with Galdós's signature, his novel *La sombra* (The Apparition), December 5 - 26, 1871, and some other contributions, although unsigned, can be specifically assigned to his authorship.[5]

Space does not permit us to mention all the periodicals to which Don Benito contributed. But simultaneously with his collaboration on *El Debate* he was involved in other journalistic enterprises. He wrote a series of fortnightly reviews of current events for *La Ilustración de Madrid* (Jan. 12, 1870 - May 30, 1872). He contributed also to the *Revista de España*, a high-level magazine founded by Albareda in 1868 and of which Galdós became the general editor from February 10, 1872 to November 13, 1873. This prestigious magazine serialized two of his novels — *El audaz* (The Bold One), 1871 - 72, and *Doña Perfecta*, 1876.

When Galdós gave up the editorship of *La Revista de España* (Nov., 1873) his decision was undoubtedly motivated by his intense activity in writing the *National Episodes*. He produced four of the novels of this collection in 1873 and was to continue at a feverish pace to the end of 1879. But there was a journalistic side even to this undertaking.

In January, 1873, a Canary Islander named Miguel Honario de Cámara y Cruz became the proprietor of a woman's magazine, *La Guirnalda* (The Garland). Its next number (January 16) contains

"Biografías de Damas Célebres Españolas" (Biographies of Celebrated Spanish Women), signed by "B. Perez Galdós," which is an introduction to a proposed series which never saw the light. In the same year two short allegories by Galdós appeared in *La Guirnalda*. Several numbers of the magazine offer sample chapters of the various *Episodes;* and the prospectus for the year 1874 announces that the subscribers to *La Guirnalda* can acquire the *National Episodes* at a reduced price not available to the general public.[7] Soon afterward (July 20, 1874) Galdós and Cámara formed a partnership, based on the equal sharing of the profits of their activities as author and publisher. For a number of years they were on intimate terms, but eventually their association broke up in a stormy quarrel.

La Guirnalda continues to push Galdós's works throughout the existence of the partnership. Its enterprising publisher conceived the idea of establishing another magazine called *El Océano*, which began publication (Jan. 4, 1879) with the announcement that it would contain "important works of our best writers, original novels of Pérez Galdós" and that subscribers would get a 10 percent discount on Galdós's works in book form. Because of its reactionary politics Galdós collaborated in *El Océano* with great reluctance.[8]

Even after Galdós had become an established and highly successful novelist, he did not completely relinquish journalism. For about ten years, beginning in 1883, he sent articles to *La Prensa* (The Press) of Buenos Aires, in which he reviewed the Spanish political, social, and literary happenings for his Latin-American readers.[9]

The incorrect or inaccurate statements about Galdós's involvement in journalism are legion, and many puzzles still remain to be solved. The chief problem is the identification of unsigned work, of which there is undoubtedly a large quantity. If Don Benito had developed a distinctive and easily recognizable style there would be no hesitation in ascribing certain anonymous articles to him. In fact there was a conventional style which was expected of those who reviewed current events. A light bantering tone was *de rigueur;* it was imitated from the French chroniclers' witty and familiar *causeries.*[10] We recognize this chatty style in Benito's weekly reviews in *La Nación* but as he becomes more experienced his writing takes on a more serious and less conventional tone. He complains of "the heavy burden of writing a review of current events every week" particularly because the miserable author "cannot deal with serious subjects" and "has left only trivial and unimportant things." Fortunately, he still has the recourse of describing picturesque types, in the manner of Mesonero Romanos.[11]

Journalism as a profession scarcely existed in Spain. A Spaniard writing in 1872 can exclaim "Journalists? There aren't any in Spain, unless an occasional political appointee out of a job merits that name, whom the owner of a paper aids with a small monthly gratification in exchange for thirty editorials, written in a uniform tone and [with] a traditional and inalterable vocabulary; and an occasional beardless writer, who attends the theater with the paper's ticket, takes notes in the gallery of the Congress, practices his French translating freely the serial [novel], and cuts out [from other papers] the short news items."[12] A couple of years earlier Benito himself speaks in the same vein, saying that young aspirants to literary fame through journalism "all run frightened from one paper to another in search of necessary sustenance which they rarely find. The greatest recompense and best termination of their weary labors is to get into a [government] office, the pantheon of all Spanish glory. . . . The unlucky fellow who does not accept this solution and insists on being a literary man pure and simple, living by his pen, could well be canonized as one of the most worthy martyrs that have tasted the bitter life in this vale of tears."[13]

Galdós had certainly made a good start as a professional journalist. Had he been able to live on his earnings, which he was not, he might never have become primarily a novelist. The economic factor in his life must not be overlooked. As soon as the novels of the *National Episodes* began selling well and were widely acclaimed, he renounced the editorship of the *Revista de España* and began to phase out his involvement with periodicals.

The apprenticeship of journalism was, however, a valuable experience for the author. His journalistic work is also very revealing of his attitudes and opinions. The modern student can see such things as his disapproval of bull fights, his love of trees and of music, his hatred of reactionary religiosity, and his disdain for the inferior architecture of Madrid churches. He condemns war as brutal and sterile and advocates tolerance and moderation.[14] Thus the biographer has many glimpses of Galdós's personality in these fugitive productions.

II   *Novels*

1. *La sombra* (The Apparition)

Galdós had spent eleven years in Madrid — educating himself, trying his hand at writing plays, above all achieving a respectable success as a journalist — when, at the age of thirty, he seemed to have found his bearings and began the production of his *National Episodes*. These historical works were not, however, his first novels. He had already published a psychological novelette and two historical narratives. When his brief tale *The Apparition* first appeared in book form (1890)[15] Galdós speaks disparagingly of it.[16] Now known as a realistic author, he feels that the fantastic character of this early work, that he places "vaguely in the year 1866 or 1867," reflects a literary taste long gone out of style. In fact there are elements of the deliberately mysterious which seem childish to the modern reader. The protagonist, Dr. Anselmo, lives in a laboratory packed with all sorts of strange objects — stuffed animals, a human skeleton, medieval armor, and the like. He carries out pseudoscientific experiments with retorts, one of which bursts, scalding his cat to a violent death.[17] This equating of the scientist with the necromancer was common enough in the romantic period[18] and was the reason for the disdain with which Galdós viewed his creation in later years.

Aside from this minor factor, Dr. Anselmo's story is a psychiatric investigation. The narrator becomes his friend and the old man tells the story of his life to him. Born into a wealthy family that lives in a palatial residence in Madrid, he inherits a diseased imagination from his father. After a dissolute youth he marries Helen, and although he scarcely knows her, since the match has been arranged by the couple's parents, Anselmo comes to love her greatly. He alternates between ecstasy and despair, for he suspects that she does not return his love.

In the picture gallery of the mansion is a painting of the Trojan Paris with Helen after her abduction. Anselmo's wife Helen admires the beauty of the figure of Paris, so when his jealousy and suspicions of his wife's infidelity take the form of hallucinations, he no longer sees the painted Paris in the picture. He is convinced that the Trojan has become his wife's lover. Then Paris appears in his room and talks to him. Anselmo tries to kill him, but the apparition is immortal. Only when his wife dies does Paris disappear.

The narrator discovers that there was a man, Alejandro, who had been paying attention to Helen. One peculiarity of Anselmo's mental state is that he has completely repressed and forgotten Alejandro until the remembrance is forced upon him. The narrator convinces him that Alejandro was the real Paris. "The logical order of the story is the following: you realized that that young man was courting your wife; you thought about it constantly, withdrew and isolated yourself in your thoughts: the fixed idea began to dominate you and finally you lost your mind" (pp. 122 - 23).

In this bare outline Dr. Anselmo's story is surely a psychiatric "case history." Whether it foreshadows Freud[19] or Pavlov,[20] it is remarkable in that it antedates both of these great psychiatrists and shows an uncommon perceptiveness on the part of its author. It is evident that Paris is a hallucination whose origin lies in Anselmo's mind. Paris himself insists that he is Anselmo's idea, that the jealous husband evoked him with his powerful imagination (81 and 121). But Anselmo is not alone in creating Paris. Helen had dreamed of an ideal lover, and even while pronouncing her loveless marriage vows she saw the vague apparition of the lover she might have had. "Her excited imagination," says Paris, "flies in search of me without ever resting" (62 - 63). Society, too, shares the responsibility for the creation of Paris, since the slightest indication of lack of harmony between the spouses gives rise to gossip (65). Society assumes that a wife is necessarily unfaithful and gleefully seizes upon any hint of a Paris-figure.

Since the apparition is, then, the result of three causes — husband, wife, and society — it can be argued that all three share in Anselmo's mental disturbance.[21] But even more striking is the assumption that almost all marriages are subject to the same disturbing factors. "That intimate suffering, that inexplicable discomfort" is Paris, who has existed since the beginning of social organization and marriage. He has taken many names, those of real or supposed seducers, the perturbers of marital felicity (55). The thought is expressed with such vehemence that it seems that Don Benito was voicing an intimate conviction.

Galdós's personal thought is evident in the many disparaging references to imagination, and it is clear that hyperdevelopment of fantasy causes Anselmo's madness. Without going outside *The Apparition* we find Dr. Anselmo saying: "For the cultivation of the arts one needs an imagination whose ardor and abundance are controlled in natural limits; an imagination which is a faculty with corresponding attributes, not, as in me, a sickness, an aberration, an organic defect" (21). What is the end result of an overabundant imagination? Although it seldom produces so clear a mental distortion as in the case of Dr. Anselmo, it does lead to a loss of contact with reality. This is to be one of the most constant themes of Galdós's work.[22] Again and again his characters allow themselves to be lured into a dream world where, Quixote-like, they take their imaginings to be real. In pages to come we shall see numerous examples of characters suffering from self-delusion because of their vivid imaginations.

What is true of Benito's fictional characters is also true of real-life Spaniards. As a young man Galdós wrote: "We are in everything dreamers who can't descend from the regions of sublime extravagance, and in literature as in politics we ride through the clouds on our winged horses as if we were not in the nineteenth century and in a corner of this old Europe which is now becoming very fond of reality. This is certain: we are outrageous idealists and we prefer to imagine rather than observe."[23] Exaggerated imagination, mysticism, illusion, daydreaming, idealism — whatever we call it, it is the greatest weakness of the Spanish mentality. Galdós shows how his modern Quixotes, his characters both male and female, project themselves into their dream worlds and how they almost invariably end in bitter disillusionment. Although they suffer defeat, he often presents their cases with humor and irony; clearly he hopes to bring about a change toward greater realism in the attitudes of his countrymen.

2. *La Fontana de Oro* (The Golden Fountain)

A splendid example of a young man with his head in the clouds is Lázaro, the protagonist of *The Golden Fountain*. "That young fellow was extremely impressionable, nervous, idealistic, disposed to live in his imagination. No one was his equal in dreaming up future incidents."[24] Lázaro directs his idealism toward politics, hoping to be a great reformer; yet he, like Don Quixote, also wanted personal glory. Up to the beginning of the action of the novel he had distinguished himself mainly as a fiery orator at the University of Zaragoza, where his speeches dealt with such abstractions as "liberty."

At the time of the action (1821) the absolutist reign of Fernando VII had been interrupted by a revolution which forced the king to abide, for three years, by the Constitution of 1812. Since Fernando had previously (in 1814) sworn to rule by the constitution and had repudiated his oath, there was a strong suspicion among liberals that the king would soon make another attempt to regain his former despotic power. The moderate liberals, although wary of the king, controlled the government; the radical opponents of tyranny gathered in secret societies and in certain coffee houses to discuss politics and especially to give passionate speeches against absolutism. One of their favorite gathering places was a café called The

Golden Fountain, where the young radicals *(exaltados)* sought to "stimulate the passions of the common people" and to "form and educate public opinion which up to that time did not exist" (8). Here Lázaro, on the night of his arrival from Aragon, gives way to the temptation to orate. His speech is a flat failure — Lázaro's first disillusionment (48 - 51); the following day he tries to harangue the mob in a street confrontation with the governmental armed forces and is thrown in jail.

Lázaro has come to Madrid, from his home town in Aragon, principally because his sweetheart, Clara, is there under the protection of Elías Orejón, Lázaro's uncle. The young man does not see his uncle until the latter visits him in jail and, to Lázaro's consternation, refuses to work for his release. In fact Elías holds ideas diametrically opposed to those of his nephew; he is an enthusiastic supporter of absolutism and a secret agent of Fernando VII. His role is to incite violence by the radicals against the moderate liberals, thus dividing and discrediting the entire constitutional party and facilitating a return to despotism.

A young army officer, Bozmediano, has fallen in love with Clara and frees Lázaro from prison in hopes of attaining her favor. But Bozmediano's continued attempts to win her dishearten Lázaro. Elías sends Clara to live with three elderly spinsters, "the three ruins," the remnants of the once noble and wealthy Porreño family. Elías and Lázaro also move to an upper floor of the same house. The youngest spinster, Paulita Porreño, suddenly drops her saintly role as a mystic and becomes passionately attracted to the young man.

During this time Lázaro has been trying to confront Bozmediano to ask an account of his relations with Clara. He only finds out that the officer and many other moderate liberals are holding secret meetings every night. (They realize that the king is trying to undermine the constitutional government of which they are the officials, and they mean to oppose his intention of reestablishing tyranny.) Elías cleverly uses Lázaro as an unwitting *agent provocateur* by encouraging him to speak again in the Golden Fountain. This time the oration is splendid, but it is twisted by Elías's men into a call for an attack on Bozmediano and the moderates. Lázaro realizes that he has been duped — a final disillusionment — and warns the moderate assembly in time to save them from the radicals.

While the young idealist is making his great speech, Clara is wandering fearfully through the inhospitable, gloomy streets of Madrid. The "three ruins" have been informed of Bozmediano's attentions toward her, and, assuming her complicity, have thrown her out of their house. She finally reaches the tavern kept by a former servant of her family; there Lázaro and Bozmediano find her. The officer, now in the role of a trusted friend, arranges for their return to Aragon, where they marry and live quietly and happily, avoiding all contact with politics.[25]

This ending, reminiscent of Voltaire's advice that "one must cultivate one's own garden," is the antidote for the inflamed imagination. Galdós felt that it contained a message applicable to the time of his novel's publication, for the troubled political situation of 1871 had notable similarities to that of 1821. Liberals and radicals were again struggling to assert their control while various candidates for the Spanish throne were waiting offstage. This book, says Don Benito, "has seemed rather opportune to me in the days through which we are passing, on account of the relationship which could be found between many events related here and some of those which are happening now. . . . This is the principal one of the reasons which have induced me to publish it" (4 - 5).

We must not think that because Lázaro renounces politics Galdós had turned his back on democratic ideals. In his book he says "A decrepit society . . . was sustaining a furious war against a healthy and vigorous society *called to the possession of the future*" ([9] italics added), and speaks of the democratic movement, begun in 1821, which has been developing with difficulty "during the last fifty years" (8). But to accomplish this ideal one must proceed with moderation, something which even Lázaro realizes when he learns that the radicals plan to exterminate the moderate leaders (163).

Lázaro, if not a flat character, is a pretty thin one. He is, in fact, *the* romantic politician and little more. Similarly, his uncle is an abstraction of servility to the tyrant. The Porreño sisters typify useless, decadent nobility.[26] It seems clear that an historical novel lends itself readily to abstract characters, for when we think of the past we are likely to view it as a struggle between impersonal forces, such as democracy and despotism. An author choosing an historical theme personifies these forces; therefore, his characters are abstract. We shall see this tendency again in some of Galdós's other early novels, even those dealing with contemporary events.

A second trend which led toward abstract characters was *costumbrismo*, already visible in Galdós's journalistic work. *Costumbrista* writers concentrated their attention on *scenes*, such as the street scenes we see in *The Golden Fountain*, and on *types*. They made it a rule not to portray individuals, but rather to offend no one by describing persons who represented a whole group, a social class, or a common psychological attitude — the miser, the pompous literary man, the fop, and so on. Their emphasis on the typical resulted in abstractions rather than individualized characters.

Although the principal actors in this novel lack complexity and psychological interest, the background of Madrid life — streets, buildings, people of the lower class — is vividly portrayed. Here we see the author's realism at work; still, we must note that his realistic details are selected to produce the audience reaction he wishes to convey. For example, the filth and stenches of the streets (5 - 6) make plausible his description of the society which would tolerate these conditions as "decrepit." The adjectives Galdós employs in his descriptions of convents — the *sad* walls, the *dirty* and *weatherbeaten* enclosure, the *ridiculous* hermitage (6) — give a hint of his anticlericalism. The realism of popular types appears not only in their physical portrayal but in their speech, where "incorrect" pronunciations are recorded (41 - 2; 151 - 52). At times this realism goes on to caricature, as when humans are compared to animals.[27]

The author also gives an air of realism to the narrative by claiming that he was a witness of some of the happenings (112 and 181) and that other facts were given him by Bozmediano, a fictitious creation whom he makes us think was a real person (165 and 181). In addition, there is historical realism in the novel. The café called "The Golden Fountain" did exist; the confrontation in which Lázaro was arrested did actually occur (the so-called Battle of the Platerías). However, there is no historical evidence for the specific uprising by which the radicals hoped to destroy Bozmediano and the gathering of moderates, although the history of the times is full of similar tumltuous actions.

Contemporary reviews of *The Golden Fountain* praise the novel's historical accuracy and the vivid descriptions of both the minor characters and the milieu in which they move. They all single out for special praise the figure of Doña Paula Porreño, who certainly is the character who shows the most remarkable development as she changes from a mystic to an impassioned lover. The novel, we conclude, has many good points but suffers from wordiness and lack of individualization of its protagonists. It paves the way for both the historical *National Episodes* and the abstract contemporary novels like *Doña Perfecta*.

3. *El Audaz* (The Bold One)

This novel, written in 1871 shortly after the appearance of *The Golden Fountain*, is so like its predecessor that it need not occupy us long. Its hero, Martín Muriel, is another idealistic political reformer. Unlike the moderate liberal Lázaro, Martín is a radical. He lives in an earlier period — the action of the novel is in 1804 — not long after the French Revolution, when the ideas of the *philosophes* were stimulating in the Spanish intelligentsia a belief in national sovereignty, the rights of man, and the abolition of the special privileges of the nobility. "Young Muriel's violent imagination was a very fertile ground in which the new ideas germinated with amazing growth" (*O.C.*, IV, 228). The events of his life intensify his hatred of the clergy and especially of the aristocracy.

Martín's father dies in jail due to the hardhearted indifference of the Count of Cerezuelo, whose estates the father had once managed. The count's daughter, Susana, treats Martín's nine-year-old brother with the same chilly indifference. So it is not surprising that Muriel rails against the "superficial aristocracy, without talent, without character, either made vile at the foot of the throne or corrupted by contact with rabble"(261). These words are spoken in the presence of Susana, who begins to take an interest in the radical. Later, Martín kidnaps her, hoping to secure the release of an imprisoned friend by an exchange of prisoners. Susana falls in love with the bold young man, follows him to Toledo, where he is leading a revolutionary coup, and commits suicide by throwing herself into the Tagus when Martín's plans fail and he is captured. He becomes insane, obsessed with the idea that he is Robespierre.

Martín was unfortunate in being born too early, when the times were not ripe for his ideas (226), when most of his followers "didn't know what they were doing nor why they were doing it (369). He falls in with other conspirators whose aim is far less lofty. Yet he has to work with these men, whose real object is their own advancement, although the discovery of their egotistic motives is a great dis-illusionment for him.

Muriel spoke of "the sovereignty of the nation," using for the first time a phrase "which afterward was to initiate a struggle lasting a half century between the hopes of modern intelligence and the in-vincible tenacity of the old social system" (371). In another place Galdós states that "the transformation about which he dreamed was a slow and difficult undertaking" (235). Here, as in *The Golden*

Fountain, is a clear message to liberals — use moderation, do not rush pell-mell after your ideals and lose contact with the realities of everyday life.

The Bold One has the same *costumbrista* realism that we saw in *The Golden Fountain,* evident partly in the pinpointing of the action in picturesque streets of Madrid, but more notably in such types as the *abate*[28] Lino Paniagua and the *manolos*[29] of the low quarters. These figures are taken from the playlets of Ramón de la Cruz, whom Galdós twice names in the course of his descriptions of these minor characters.[30] Goya's painting also contributed to some descriptions, especially to the *fête champêtre* of the aristocratic group (263 - 65).

There is probably an influence of Dickens, specifically of *Barnaby Rudge,* because the anti-Catholic uprising of the populace and the burning of Newgate prison have similarities to Galdós's riots in Toledo and the burning of the building of the Inquisition. The fact that there is no historical basis for Don Benito's Toledan episode, in other words, that it is a purely fictitious invention of the author, lends greater credence to his having modeled it on a literary prototype.

In conclusion we repeat that *The Bold One* restates the problem and the message of *The Golden Fountain,* its chief difference being that Martín Muriel is a radical liberal while Lázaro is a relatively timid moderate.

CHAPTER 4

The National Episodes

I *Galdós and History*

IN both *The Golden Fountain* and *The Bold One* Don Benito
speaks of the democratic movement which had been developing
haltingly "for the last fifty years," giving rise to the events of the
present. The past holds the present in germ; history is the slow in-
cubation of vital change. In his *National Episodes* this notion is expressed frequently, for example: "history, gradually, through the
smooth birth of effects in the womb of causes, and these effects in
their turn being causes that engender new effects..." (*O.C.*, II,
1329b).

According to Don Benito change is inevitable, but we must not try
to anticipate its arrival. It was the tragedy of Muriel — and to a
lesser extent of Lázaro — to try to force social change before the
fullness of time. A willingness to wait, not to demand greater change
than the time will allow, is *moderation* — Galdós's message to his
contemporaries, who he hopes will learn from the examples of the
past. In one of his *National Episodes*, Salvador Monsalud (who lived
in the 1820s and '30s) says: "My ideal is far off. Time still keeps it so
hidden that one cannot catch a glimpse of it anywhere here. But it
will come, and, although *we* are not to see it as a reality worthy to be
admired, it consoles us to look forward in thought into an obscure
future and to contemplate the fine novelties of our grandsons' Spain.
Meanwhile, I can't be enthusiastic because I don't believe in the
present. . . . I'll dream about the distant future of our country, very
distant in truth" (323 - 24). Liberal ideals, yes; but violence to
achieve these ideals, no.

The conception of history as progress goes back to the eighteenth-
century *philosophes*, and it became the ideal of the liberal middle
class. After the appearance of Darwin's *Origin of Species* (1859) an
association of progress and evolution was inevitable. Galdós chose

the bourgeoisie — scarcely existing in Spain before 1850 because of the turbulence of the Napoleonic and Carlist wars — as the center of his hopes for social change. "It is today the basis of social order." It "determines the political movement," administers, teaches, gives the nation both the good and the bad of modern civilization, "the great innovators and the great libertines, the ambitious geniuses and the ridiculous vanities; it controls commerce, one of the great manifestations of our century, and it possesses the key to finance, a powerful element of present-day life."[1] Galdós not only chooses the middle class as the focus of his literary work but sees in its growth the hope for a new classless society in which social justice will be finally achieved.

He feels that the bourgeoisie will recruit new members from both the aristocracy and the plebs and that the idealism of the best members of the nobility will combine with the materialistic strength of the latter, or, at least, that the rough virtues of the common people will be polished by the sophistication of the upper classes. His theme is best illustrated in some of his plays where his symbolism is all too apparent. The Duchess of San Quintín marries an intelligent young engineer, a man far below her rank, thus merging the classes. In one symbolic scene she prepares dough for cookies, into which must go ordinary flour but also select elements, spices, which combine with the flour to produce something superior to either element alone.[2] Again, in another play, *La loca de la casa* (The Madcap), the mystical daughter of a ruined factory owner gives up her intention of taking the veil to save her father from bankruptcy by marrying an enriched former servant. His crude materialism yields to her idealism when she persuades him to endow a hospital.

Marriages between nobles and commoners also occur in Galdós's novels.[3] Even toward the end of his literary career he can still look to a fusion of the upper and lower classes. "The so-called middle class, which still doesn't have a positive existence, is just a formless agglomeration of individuals proceeding from the upper and lower categories, the product, we may say, of the decomposition of both families: of the plebeian which rises; of the aristocratic, which descends. . . . This enormous mass without a distinctive character of its own . . . will end by absorbing the deteriorated remains of the opposed classes, the depositories of elemental sentiments. When this comes to pass there will take place in the heart of this chaotic mass a fermentation from which will come social forms which we cannot divine, vigorous elements we are unable to define in the confusion and perplexity in which we are living."[4] Galdós had little sympathy for the aristocracy, although he did attribute sophistication to the class and idealism to some of its members. Frequently he dwells on the dissolute customs and grasping, uncharitable egotism of the nobles.

Benito's thought with respect to the common man is sharply polarized. At times the ignorant, superstitious rabble, especially when led by unscrupulous demagogues, can run wild, burning and murdering. But the lower class is by no means always a mob. It can fight valiantly for the patriotic cause.[5] Its native good sense, its humor, its loyalty and trustworthiness make it "the quarry of Spanish virtues." The slowness of its advance toward middle-class status disappoints Galdós, who, toward the end of his career, looks back on the period of the Restoration (1875 - 98) with disillusionment. Liberalism is discredited in Spain as elsewhere; the disaster of the Spanish-American War has deprived the notion of historical progress of credibility. But Galdós continues to believe in the Spanish people, who, despite their long history, have remained in a state of childhood, with many good qualities still in germ. Their great need is education; their great antagonists are the political bosses and the Jesuits.[6]

Soon after the declarations of this interview Galdós changed allegiances, switching from liberalism (he had served as a liberal representative in the Cortes ["Congress"] from 1886 to 1890) to republicanism. He was elected as a representative of the republicans in 1907 and 1914. His concern for the common people led him to sympathize with the reform program of Joaquín Costa and with the socialist leader Pablo Iglesias.[7] But the experience with republicanism was also disillusioning. The leaders of the party were not the idealists that the novelist expected to find. At the very end of his productive life, thoroughly disillusioned, Galdós laments bitterly the loss of idealism in the middle class.[8] Marxist critics, seeing the middle class as the great oppressor of the proletariat and liberalism as a hypocritical doctrine designed to further selfish ends, have accused Galdós of knowingly supporting bourgeois ideals because of fear of a working-class revolution.[9] Hence it has been necessary to dwell here on his unswerving belief in, and hope for, the betterment of the plebs.

Two other thoughts about history are prominent in the Spaniard's historical novels. First, there is the notion that history is much more than the record of great events and great men. "If in History there were nothing but battles; if its only actors were celebrated personages, how little it would be! It is in the slow and almost always sorrowful life of society, in what all do and what each one does."[10] This idea leads us back to the importance of the common people, as Don Benito shows in his account of the death of a minor character who died leaving "a scarcely visible trace, hardly perceptible in the field of anonymous history, that is to say, that history which could and ought to be written without personages, without great figures, only with selections from the elemental protagonist which is the rugged and blessed common man, the nation, the collective nameless individual."[11]

The second idea has to do with historical necessity and its cause. If the course of events is predetermined, if, as Galdós says, "it had to be because of ineluctable law," is it God or Fate which controls what is to happen? Most frequently Providence is invoked in the earlier historical works while Fate takes over in the later ones. While Providence is occasionally cognate with Heaven or even God, it is more commonly a vague force, idealistic or spiritual in nature, easily confused with Fate when the latter works toward a good end. For example José Fago, meditating on the possibility of the death of the wounded Carlist general Zumalacárregui, decides that his death is inevitable. "It is a law which has to be carried out." The man who wounded him is an "instrument of Fate" and his death is part of "historical logic. God has taught me how to recognize opportuneness in History and when it is good that evil should occur."[12]

It is evident that Galdós had a definite, not very original, conception of history as a very slow but inevitable development toward a more perfect social state. The most personal portion of his thought was the rather naive hope that the then embryonic Spanish middle class would ultimately absorb both the decadent nobility and the fundamentally good but often misled lower classes.

II *The* National Episodes *and Money Problems*

Galdós began to publish his first series of ten historical novels in 1873. They proved to be extremely popular, so that for the first time the thirty-year-old author could live on his own earnings, an economic reality usually overlooked by biographers. In the year preceding the beginning of this task Galdós began to contribute to *La Guirnalda,* and on July 20, 1874, as indicated above, the publisher and the author entered a partnership, by which they were to share equally the profits of their work. The first ten volumes were completed by March, 1875, each one written in about two months.

Without pausing Galdós began a second series, which, despite interruptions caused by the writing of four novels on the contemporary
scene, he finished at the end of 1879. In the epilogue of this series he
swears that he will never write another historical novel.

By this time Don Benito's economic problem seemed to be solved
for the rest of his life. Between 1874 and 1896, the period of his
association with Cámara, his average annual income was 14,272
pesetas, which becomes meaningful when compared to the salaries
of government ministers (15,000 pesetas) and the wages of plumbers,
carpenters, and masons (3.75 pesetas a day).[13] He wanted to use his
financial independence to write contemporary novels, works which
would give him immortality. Even while writing the Second Series
he was not satisfied with the *National Episodes*, for he says that he
wants to write a *great* book "after so many trivial little works as I
have sent forth throughout the world."[14] Undoubtedly he also
wished to imitate his two early idols, Balzac and Dickens, both of
whom combined literary excellence with handsome earnings, and to
rival the new supernovelist, Zola, whose scandalous *L'Assommoir*
(1878) was to move the Frenchman to the first rank of authors and of
literary entrepreneurs.

But the hopes of continued financial ease were not realized. The
contemporary novels, literarily superior to the *National Episodes*,
did not have the same popularity and did not sell as well as the
earlier works.[15] Then family debts fell heavily on the author. His
oldest brother, Domingo, died in 1870 leaving debts which were not
fully paid until 1886 or even later.[16] Galdós also supported sisters,
nephews, and his sister-in-law; the family demands on him were
heavy. Appeals to his charity also drained his purse. Finally, his only
great personal indulgence, the construction of a house overlooking
the sea on the outskirts of Santander, was extremely costly.[17] There
followed a quarrel with his partner after which Galdós set himself up
as his own publisher. Heavily burdened by debts to Cámara, to his
lawyer, and to moneylenders, he needed to recoup his fortune by
producing and selling rapidly.

So Don Benito returned to the *National Episodes*. The first
volume of the Third Series is dated "April-May, 1898"; the last
"September-October, 1900." Ten volumes in two years and seven
months! Yet these works lacked the broad patriotic appeal of the
earlier episodes. Even Galdós's friends found their action dragged
and that some characters were too abstract.[18] In any case, they did
not provide the solution to his financial problems.

The year 1901 marked the triumphal production of the play *Elec-*

tra, acted not only in Madrid but in numerous provincial cities and throughout Spanish America. It was Galdós's greatest financial success over the short haul, although a number of his novels gave him greater returns over a period of years. The immediate effect of the triumph was that Don Benito gave up writing the *National Episodes* during this year; in fact, he produced nothing but *Electra* in 1901.

But his debts were still not liquidated. A loan of 8,000 pesetas, taken from a certain Encarnación Gómez, runs from 1898 up to January, 1904, and cost Galdós 960 pesetas annually in interest.[19] Again the weary author took up his pen and turned out another ten *Episodes* between 1902 and 1907. Then, as his strength failed and blindness overtook him he struggled with a fifth series, of which only six were completed, the last three after he went completely blind. During this period his activity in republican politics took much of his time, money, and physical strength. He entered his last years a poor man.

The *National Episodes* are clearly related to Galdós's financial status, first at the beginning of his career, when they gave him independence, and later, when they failed to put him back on a sound footing. To see them as purely literary productions, isolated from the realities of the workaday world, is to fail to understand their significance for the author himself.

III   *The First Series* [20]

This series, by far the most popular, deals with events from 1805 — the battle of Trafalgar — to 1813, the end of the Napoleonic invasion of Spain. Many of its tomes concentrate on some military action, such as the sieges of Zaragoza and Gerona, the battles of Bailén and Los Arapiles, as well as the above-mentioned naval battle of Trafalgar. Throughout the series the struggle of the Spanish people, for once united by their resistance to French domination, is the principal theme; hence, the ensemble is rightly said to have an epic tone.

These lofty events are narrated by Gabriel Araceli, an old man who in his youth took part in all but one of the occurrences.[21] He starts life as a street urchin in Cádiz, becomes a cabin boy at Trafalgar, a page in the royal court, and finally a soldier participating in many of the wide-flung campaigns. He discovers patriotic ideals and moves upward into the solid middle class. Galdós calls him a "redeemed picaro," and hopes that poor boys in modern times will follow his example.[22]

The fictitious element involves Gabriel's love for Inés, the natural daughter of Countess Amaranta, a girl far above the hero's social position, which poses a seemingly unsurmountable problem. Since the solution cannot be worked out until the tenth volume, the action of the plot is necessarily very slow and episodic. Much of the time the lovers are separated; in some volumes Inés is mentioned only briefly. Of course, many subplots help to sustain reader interest.

The only character who develops is the hero; the rest of the multitude of fictitious or real persons are presented as types. Thus the author succeeds in symbolizing the social forces of the period — the degenerate nobles at the court, the supporters of the French, the popular types of the common people. Often a whole group of patriots act together as a collective protagonist. The great men who appear in the novels usually have only minor roles.

Much is known about Galdós's historical sources for this, as well as other series. His personal library contained many books of history, often profusely marked. He tells us that he interviewed survivors of the events; for example, the last living participant in the battle of Trafalgar. But not many eye witnesses remained for happenings so long ago. Not until he began the Second Series did he have the invaluable aid of Mesonero Romanos, whose prodigious memory was an archive on which he could draw.[23]

The style of the First as well as the Second Series is not highly individualized. It is a direct narration in everyday language, ornamented only by racy popular phrases and relieved from monotony by dialogue in which each character speaks in the language of his social rank. Much humor appears in ironical descriptions, and often reminiscences of Cervantes's phraseology strike our ear. Linguistically these episodes deserve the qualification of realism, "a characteristic expression of bourgeois society."[24]

IV   *The Second Series*

These ten works cover Spanish history from the defeat of Napoleon (1813) to the death of King Fernando VII (1834). It is a period marked not by a united struggle against a foreign invader, but by internecine conflict between absolutists, headed by the king, and the liberals, who looked forward to a constitutional monarchy. The splitting of the body politic into opposed factions, often referred to by the phrase "the two Spains," began at that time and continues even today.

Galdós abandons the technique of a single, first-person narrator used in the previous series and becomes the omniscient author in seven *Episodes*. Two others are told by Juan Bragas and a third by Genara, both of whom have principal roles in the series. Instead of centering the plot in the adventures of one hero, he uses a group of four protagonists whose lives are interrelated. The chief one of the four is Salvador Monsalud who, in the first volume of the series is a soldier in the forces defending Joseph Bonaparte, but who becomes an ardent liberal and finally in disillusionment withdraws from political activity, seeing in it nothing but mistakes, corruption of new systems, and noble ideas bastardized by bad faith (see above, p. 43).

Juan Bragas is the political opportunist who always has a bureaucratic job no matter what government is in power. Galdós depicts him with satirical humor. The third male protagonist is Carlos Navarro, alias Garrote, the leader of a cruel band of reactionary *guerrilleros* and the rival of Monsalud for the affections of Genara. This beautiful, highly independent, passionate woman scoffs at moral strictures and puts her happiness above all other considerations. She is first Monsalud's fiancée, then marries Garrote, then has an affair with her first love.

All four principal characters are from the same small town in northern Spain, which gives a rational basis for intertwining the threads of their lives. But the major part of the action takes place in Madrid, not, as in the First Series, in other parts of the country. Each one of the four principal characters acts within a segment of the society of their times, so that taken all together, their careers give the author the opportunity to sketch for us the national sociopolitical scene. Juan Bragas takes us into the cynical world of bureaucrats. Genara conspires with the supporters of Fernando VII, while Monsalud joins the plots of the Masons against absolutism. Garrote, convinced that his reactionary world is already as good as destroyed, is determined to die with it, like a captain going down with his ship. He obviously symbolizes the society which Galdós disliked just as Monsalud represents the burgeoning future. The symbolism is especially apparent when Garrote and Salvador discover, after years of mutual hatred, that they are sons of the same father. The theme of "the two Spains," the division of families, pitting brother against brother, is clearly visible.

Since these characters represent social groups they must necessarily be typical. Bragas and Garrote especially appear as types, whereas Genara and Monsalud have many individualizing traits. The former's strong will makes her go directly and impulsively after the objects of her desires; the latter is not always the invariable liberal. He is capable of helping his political adversaries, of easing his half-brother's death, and of securing the freedom of the absolutist Gil de la Cuadra, whose daughter Soledad he later marries. In short, he is swayed by human emotions, which cause him to react not as a consistent, typical liberal but as a self-contradicting individual. His ultimate disillusionment with active politics has already been quoted (page 43).

Taken as a whole the Second Series has greater fictional but less historical interest than the First. The author, no longer bound by the device of the first-person narrator, can use his omniscience to great advantage in the portrayal of his characters. He uses ironical humor well, often bordering on caricature. But the patriotic fervor of the struggle against the foreign invader has disappeared.

A gap of nineteen years (1879 - 1898) separates the Second from the Third Series of *National Episodes*. We shall return to the *Episodes* in their chronological place.

CARNEGIE LIBRARY
LIVINGSTONE COLLEGE
SALISBURY, N. C. 28144

CHAPTER 5

The First Contemporary Novels

I *The Background*

AS early as 1870 Galdós had made a clear declaration of his ideas about the Spanish novel. He said it should be a reflection of all that is good and bad in the middle class, which dominates modern society. The evident implication is that the novel should deal with the contemporary scene, not history, and Don Benito states this notion more clearly two years later: "Novels should be *realistic, Spanish* [in subject], and *contemporary* [my italics], although this last cannot be maintained without a certain narrowness of view."[1] In theory Galdós believed that the historical novel was less worthy than the contemporary, although he was on the verge of producing his *National Episodes* when he penned these last words. No doubt his intention of teaching his compatriots the lessons of history motivated his turn away from contemporary subjects.

But as he wrote his First Series the political structure around him was changing with kaleidoscopic rapidity. The constitutional monarch, Amadeo de Saboya, whom Galdós had supported in the columns of *El Debate*, abdicated, saying that "Spaniards are ungovernable;" a republic took over for a year (1873); finally, the Bourbon dynasty was restored in the person of Alfonso XII. A period of political calm ensued, based on the agreement of Liberals and Conservatives to share alternately the direction of the government. Concessions had to be made to both sides. The Conservatives gained a clause in the new constitution which rescinded the freedom of conscience that had been established by the Revolution of 1868 and imposed Catholicism as the national religion and as a part of the educational curriculum. Galdós sees the new intolerance as an exacerbation of the question which perturbs bourgeois society, for he feels that the religious problem is of supreme importance.

The year 1876 is a milestone, politically for the promulgation of the new constitution and for the end of another Carlist war, and in Galdós's writings for his turning to the contemporary scene and the theme of religious conflict. He is to write three thesis novels, which attack savagely the intolerance of the traditionalists now enshrined in the new constitution.

II   Doña Perfecta *(April, 1876)*

Pepe Rey, a young engineer "of lofty ideas and immense love of science," which he has studied in Germany and England (*O.C.*, IV, 409), symbolizes modern, progressive civilization. At his father's instigation he goes to Orbajosa, a remote and backward cathedral town, with the idea of meeting his cousin Rosario and considering a possible marriage with her. There he clashes with his aunt, Rosario's mother, Doña Perfecta, whose subtle, hypocritically concealed opposition is gradually revealed. She has an ally in the priest Don Inocencio. Because Pepe is very outspoken and lacking in tact, he argues with the priest, criticizes church art and music, and then finds himself opposed in numerous ways — by lawsuits concerning lands he owns in the region, by the loss of government commissions to survey the area for mining and irrigation projects, and ultimately in his intention to marry Rosario, whom he has come to love. When Pepe Rey tries to elope with her, Doña Perfecta gives the order to kill him to one of her henchmen. After Pepe's death Rosario becomes insane and must be confined to an asylum; Doña Perfecta gives herself over to unending religious activities.

A secondary plot concerns the hope of María Remedios, Don Inocencio's niece and housekeeper, of marrying her son Jacinto to Rosario.[2] Because of her desire to catch the young lady's fortune for her son she aids all attacks against Pepe. But the latter receives unexpected help from an army officer whose company is sent to Orbajosa to discourage the uprising of guerrilla bands.

The conflict between modern thought, represented by Pepe Rey, and reactionary traditionalism, personified in Doña Perfecta and Don Inocencio, is actually much larger than a personal confrontation. It is the city versus the country, Madrid versus the province, the central government (represented particularly by the national armed forces) versus regionalism (represented by guerrilla bands), and religious tolerance versus Neo-Catholicism.

The author gives ironical treatment to Orbajosa and its inhabitants. The surrounding desolate fields rejoice in such names as *Valleameno* ("Pleasant Valley"), *Cerro de los Lirios* ("Hill of

Lillies"), and *Valdeflores* ("Vale of Flowers"). Orbajosa itself — according to some, the *Urbs augusta* of the Romans — presents an aspect of "ruin and death rather than of prosperity and life," a sepulchre (*O.C.*, IV, 407), a city whose name may derive from *Orbajosa* ("city of garlic"). The same irony gives rise to the names Doña "Perfecta" and Don "Inocencio."

For the Orbajosans one of the chief reasons for combating the central government is a religious one. They believe that Madrid is destroying the church, that many of its buildings in the capital have been torn down, and that priests receive all manner of insults (469). Orbajosa, in their minds, is the champion of Catholicism.

There is little doubt that *Doña Perfecta* is Galdós's reaction to the intolerance that was expressed in the Constitution of 1876, which was being formulated during the preceding year and was promulgated while the novel was appearing in installments. The book is a vigorous statement of the author's views on the *negative* force of misunderstood religion. The last words of the novel, "[This] is all we can say for the moment about people who seem good and are not," show clearly that Galdós had no sympathy for the hypocrisy of the Orbajosans.

Yet we may ask if Doña Perfecta is all bad and Pepe Rey is all good. Is the novel then a melodrama, as has been argued?[3] Or does it follow the pattern of the Greek tragedy, in which the hero's tragic flaw (Pepe's tactlessness) brings about his downfall?[4] While we cannot deny that Galdós wished to portray hypocritical, Neo-Catholic religiosity in a highly unfavorable light, we must also agree that Pepe Rey helped to bring on himself his tragic end, precisely by a lack of moderation, which was the theme of Galdós's early historical novels.

Clarín quotes Galdós as saying that he had no plan and that "I began *Doña Perfecta* without knowing how I was to develop the subject. I wrote it in spurts, I mean, in pieces, as it was coming out [in the *Revista de España*]."[5] To this we can only say that the novel is remarkably well organized — save for the abandoned original ending (see n. 2) — and that it gives the impression of a work structured in advance. Galdós tended always to conceal his creative process and to give the impression that he just dashed off his novels. If he was influenced by Turgenev's *Fathers and Sons* in preparing *Doña Perfecta*,[6] as seems likely, he must have given more thought to his plan than he admits.

Doña Perfecta continues to be one of the most read and highly esteemed of Galdós's novels. It is by no means his greatest work, but it stirs up some of the author's passionate reaction to hypocrisy and backward intolerance in its readers.

III   Gloria (*Vol. I, December 1876; Vol. II, May 1877*)

In essence *Gloria* is the story of two lovers separated by religion. The Jewish hero, Daniel Morton, is shipwrecked on the north coast of Spain and given shelter in the home of Don Juan de Lantigua. This conservative, unquestioning Catholic gentleman is the father of Gloria, who without knowing Daniel's religion, falls in love with him. The Lantigua family assumes that Morton must be a Protestant since he is an English citizen. Gloria and Daniel can see no radical difference in their beliefs and feel that it is only man-made accretions to the fundamental spirit of religion which cause conflict between the sects and keep them apart.

Only after they make love (leading in due time to the birth of a son) does Daniel reveal the momentous fact that he is a Jew. One can hardly exaggerate the anti-Jewish bias of nineteenth-century Spaniards. Gloria's father dies from the shock; she herself now joins the forces of intolerance and declares she can never marry Daniel unless he becomes a Christian.

In the second volume Daniel returns from England when he hears that Gloria has given birth to his son. He finds the entire town, even those persons he has aided, adamantly set against him. Gloria has fallen into a kind of stupor and her health is progressively worsening. Her Aunt Serafinita is urging her to renounce her child and enter a convent, while her Uncle Buenaventura proposes a compromise solution. He meets with Daniel and suggests a feigned conversion to Catholicism followed by marriage to Gloria. With the greatest reluctance, because of his sincere faith and his knowledge that his family would ostracize him, Daniel accepts Buenaventura's plan.

But there is a Jewish intolerance quite as strong as the Catholic variety. Esther Spinoza, Daniel's mother, arrives in town, ingratiates herself with the authorities, and has her son arrested on the charge of stealing funds from the family. Before he can be transported to England, he and Gloria meet beside their son's cradle. The baby is in the care of a woman who lives next to a village church and from the church they can hear the Easter service, the joyous resurrection and rebirth. At the moment when the priest intones *Gloria, in excelsis Deo*, Gloria dies. Four years later Daniel also dies after losing his sanity trying to devise "a new religion, the single religion, the religion of the future" (*O.C.*, IV, 678). Their little son, Jesús, remains as "the personification of Humanity emancipated from religious antagonisms by virtue of love" (679).

The lines just quoted leave us no doubt about Galdós's didactic intention. If the spirit of all religions has love, even of one's enemies, as a basic tenet, why have hatred and intolerance developed between the various faiths? The blame must be placed not on God but on man, who has corrupted the essential religious spirit. In this belief Galdós is following the attitude of the Krausists, whose philosophy emphasized tolerance of all religions and the pruning from them of all man-made, extraneous doctrines. While in *Doña Perfecta* the author was concerned only with Catholic intolerance of modern ideas, in *Gloria* he broadens his scope. Both Catholicism and Judaism are flagellated for their identical lack of universal love; by implication all religions come under the same indictment.

In a statement quoted by Clarín, Galdós says that "*Gloria* was the work of an enthusiasm of a fortnight. It occurred to me while walking through the Puerta del Sol, between Montera Street and the Universal Café; and it occurred *suddenly* with my seeing clearly all the first volume. The second volume is artificial and was composed with difficulty. Would that I had never written it! X . . . was to blame for my writing this second part because he told me (these devilish critics!) that I ought to bring out the consequences of the thesis and exhaust the theme."[7] Today we know a good deal more about the circumstances of the composition of the novel. In a letter to Pereda, Don Benito tells him that he is taking up again a novel written a few years previously (see p. 47). The manuscript of *Gloria* has been found and on the back of its pages we can see the very different primitive version as well as part of a second preliminary draft.[8] We can only conclude that the sudden formulation of the plan of the first part was a moment of crystallization, when all elements of the first volume fell into place.[9] Using some of the pages of the rejected second draft and working feverishly he could finish the first volume in a fortnight.

The most important conclusion from this discovery is that we must not look on Galdós as an improviser, an impression he liked to give in order to shield his creative process from public view. We must see him as a conscientious, painstaking literary artisan, something which is true not only of him but of almost all great writers.

Gloria is then a thesis novel, much more temperate in tone than *Doña Perfecta*, but like it emphasizing the bad effects of religious intolerance. Although there is still a certain abstractness in the protagonists, they are much more human than Pepe Rey and Doña Perfecta, in whom social forces are personified. Gloria develops from a sprightly girl capable of independent thought to a stunned martyr, crushed by oppressive fanaticism. Daniel, too, shows human traits. His inner conflict — his religion versus his love for Gloria and his desire to treat her honorably — is no mere abstraction but a source of spiritual torment. Don Juan de Lantigua was not a complete fanatic. "In practical life, Lantigua got along benignly with men of ideas the most contrary to his own, and even had [among them] intimate friends whom he loved" (504). Only in matters of religion was he intransigent.

So we can say that *Gloria* represents a considerable advance over *Doña Perfecta* in the plausibility of its characters. Only secondary ones embody Galdós's anticlerical feelings — the priest Silvestre Romero and the hypocritical Neo-Catholic politician Rafael del Horro.

IV   Marianela (1877)

Gloria was not well received by the Neo-Catholics[10] and apparently Don Benito felt he should vary his production with a noncontroversial novel in order to regain favor with his readers. In any case he soon brought out a work, usually described as an idyll, in which a physically stunted girl dies from hopeless love. Marianela is an abused, neglected orphan who serves a blind boy (Pablo Penáguilas) as a guide. Before Dr. Golfín restores his sight, Pablo is convinced that her body must be just as beautiful as her soul; but once he has his vision he falls in love with his beautiful cousin Florentina. Marianela hides from him and eventually dies.

This novel fictionalizes the positivistic philosophy of Auguste Comte, which became popular in Madrid a few months before Galdós composed his work.[11] Comte felt that mankind has gone through three stages in development — the theological, in which reality is explained through myths and the imagination is dominant; the metaphysical, when without observing reality man tries by reason alone to explain his environment; and finally the positivistic stage, which amounts to scientific deduction of natural laws from observed reality. To this scheme Comte added a notion of a new religion, "the heaven of the Virgin Mary."

Professor Joaquín Casalduero[12] has shown how Marianela's imaginative explanation of nature (stars, flowers, etc.) corresponds to

Comte's theological stage. Galdós clearly states that she is a survival of primitive mankind. Pablo Penáguila possesses a highly developed ability to think logically, but his blindness isolates him from much of reality. He is the metaphysical man, representing a stage which Comte regarded as transitory and of short duration; hence he must gain complete contact with reality along with his sight. Of course Dr. Golfín is the positivist, and Florentina, often called "the Immaculate" or "the Virgin," is related to Comte's religion of the Virgin Mary.

Marianela is then an "abstract" novel, obviously modeled on a philosophic system. But in addition to Comte's underlying system there is a strong influence from Goethe's *Wilhelm Meister*, especially visible in the similarities between Mignon and the Spanish girl. Mignon, the physically underdeveloped child-woman, loves Wilhelm and dies heartbroken when he falls in love with another woman. There is also a marked similarity between this Galdosian work and a type of late romantic novel which stressed sentimental humanitarianism. Specifically Victor Hugo's *Les Misérables* and Eugène Sue's *Le Juif errant* have heroines physically handicapped or oppressed by society. They inspire the same tearful pity that Marianela awakens in the reader.[13]

Criticism of society's indifference to poverty and its unwillingness to provide even rudimentary education or training for girls like Marianela is one message of the book. A secondary one is that just as Marianela must die when Pablo gains a complete contact with the real world, so imagination must give way to scientific thought, or at least it must be kept under strict control. Otherwise we are plunged into an unreal world of fantasy, the trend which Don Benito saw as a chief weakness of his compatriots. Thus, the novel is not merely a lyrical rhapsody, as sometimes claimed, but does have a clear social message. It is Galdós's only work in a strongly sentimental tone, a peculiarity which we feel must be related to his sources of inspiration, especially the pathetic figure of Mignon.

V La familia de León Roch (1878 - 1879)

After dropping religious, although not social, criticism in *Marianela*, Galdós returned to the theme of the nefarious results of misunderstood religion in his next novel. The eponymous hero makes the mistake of marrying the wrong girl. Pepa Fúcar, his wealthy but physically unattractive childhood playmate, is the one he rejects for the beautiful María de Tellería. He assumes he can form a perfect wife out of the latter, endowing her with his philosophic and scientific outlook, but he finds an insurmountable obstacle in her shallow, albeit unyielding, religiosity. Divorced spiritually although not legally (an impossibility in Spain) León moves out of his home to a house next door to Pepa's magnificent estate.

In the interim Pepa, piqued by León's rejection, married Federico Cimarra, a scoundrel whose shady financial dealings led him to Cuba, where he was lost, and apparently died, in a shipwreck. Pepa's little daughter, Monina, adored by León, is the cause of reestablished comradeship and eventually chaste love between the two grown-ups. Gossips spread the rumor that Monina is León's daughter. When this word reaches María she is fired by intense jealousy. She puts off her sackcloth garments, symbols of her religiosity, dons her finest, and rushes to confront León, intending to win him back with her beauty. However, a sudden heart attack brings her to the point of death. Before she dies news that Federico Cimarra is alive and back in Madrid destroys the possibility of marriage for León and Pepa. Pepa listens only to the commands of love and suggests that they flee together to another country; but León hears only the dictates of his conscience and acts in complete harmony with his Krausistic beliefs. "As for me, this woman belongs to me; I consider her mine by the law of my heart. . . . Let this daring rebellion remain in my mind and not become reality. Let the man who cannot transform the world and root out its errors respect them" (*O.C.*, IV, 951).

Here we have the first expression of the conflict between *natural* law and *social* law, love and marriage, which is to be prominent in such works as *Fortunata and Jacinta*. In this case social law triumphs, although a few years later the author gives what is in effect a less austere and less virtuous ending to *La familia de León Roch* (León Roch's Family). The protagonist of *Lo prohibido* (Forbidden Fruit) meets Cimarra at a reception and learns that he has "resigned himself to his wife's living materially with León Roch in Pau" (*O.C.*, IV, 1721). By the time he penned these words Don Benito had become a naturalist and must have felt that León's virtue was not in keeping with this new literary orientation. But when he created his personage he conceived him as a freethinking philosopher and natural scientist, indoctrinated with the rationalistic humanism of Krause.[14] Like the Krausists he is "one of those products of the University, the Atheneum, and the School of Mines," (762 - 63) and like them he is misunderstood and ridiculed, regarded as an atheist even by his wife.

Again following the Krausist doctrine, León "became enamored from his early youth with an ideal for life, which was a calm, virtuous existence, formed of love and study . . ." (793). Thinking that he has made a logical decision to marry María he exclaims that he will be able to form the character of his wife and make her in his image and likeness (773 - 74). Galdós comments on León's self-delusion: "Did he see in his wife anything more than an extraordinary beauty? What role did his heart play in that delirium of love? It would be amusing if the man who boasted so much of having enslaved his imagination should allow himself to be swept away by it" (777). Obviously León has parted company with reality. His noble ideal fails in practice because he saw an imaginary woman in María. The same confusion of dreams and reality is visible in María's twin brother, Luis Gonzaga, a young Jesuit novice who dreams of becoming a saint and "cultivates his sickness as one cares for a growing flower" (809) and finally dies "contravening natural laws." Galdós thinks of him as a Quixote of religion and uses him to underline and intensify the character of his twin sister. He exhorts her to give up worldly pomp, fine clothes, and all but a perfunctory consideration for her husband (815 - 16). So María, like her brother, assumes an exaggerated religious posture until jealousy awakens the woman in her.

León brings María's confessor, Father Paoletti, to María's bedside as she is dying. She greets the priest "with a joyful cry." She looked at both men affectionately, then "held out a hand to each one. That movement . . . was the compendium of her life and might even be the synthesis of this book in respect to the lady" (902). Shortly afterward the priest uses the plural in saying that "María will live *for us*. That plural," adds Galdós, "was the most cruel sarcasm that León had ever heard from human lips in his whole life" (905). It brings into the work the subtheme of the conflict of the husband and the confessor, a favorite topic of anticlerical writers.[15]

The other members of the Tellería family — León's family by his marriage — are all prodigal spendthrifts and dip into León's pocket whenever their own is empty. Leopoldo, one of María's brothers, is a sickly society playboy; another brother, Gustavo, is a Neo-Catholic politician. These two young men and their father are all profligates; the mother of the family is not much better. She will reappear in later Galdosian novels.

León Roch's Family is the last of the early series of contemporary novels, all produced during the time when Galdós was still writing the *National Episodes.* This novel marks a considerable advance over the others in respect to realism. The locale of the action in the others is in every case an imaginary one, although clearly a composite of elements taken from reality. This last work also begins in an imaginary place, an unidentifiable spa in the Basque country, but then the scene of action shifts to Madrid and its suburbs. While Galdós does not often name specific streets and squares in this novel, a constant practice in his later works, it does move in the ambient of reality.

The greater reality of the setting corresponds to a new realism — a first hint of naturalism — in some of the descriptive passages. As for the principal characters we must admit that they are not strongly individualized. To some extent their typification makes them abstractions. León is the Krausist freethinker in everything, María the church-dominated woman. Neither one surprises us with some thought or action out of character. The secondary personages are all flat characters, but many of them will reappear in later novels, just as Doña Perfecta and Cayetano Polentinos from *Doña Perfecta* and Celepín from *Marianela* reappear in this one. Nevertheless, the author shows all his creatures in many insignificant little acts that give them a greater humanity than can be claimed for Pepe Rey or Doña Perfecta. We shall soon see that winds of naturalism were blowing from France into Spain while *León Roch's Family* was being written. This movement may well have left its first traces in this novel of Galdós.

VI *Relationship of the Historical and Contemporary Novels*

We have remarked that the historical novel lends itself to the abstraction of characters (see p. 39). Other than the "great men" of history, few individuals appear in the chronicles. On the other hand all the social and political forces are recorded, and to novelize them personages must be endowed with the typical traits of the various movements. The contemporary scene also has its conflicting forces and their antagonism leads naturally to the thesis novel and, in turn, to the symbolizing of the opposed attitudes in "abstract" characters. The habit of personifying historical forces is easily transferred to modern times, which is precisely what Galdós did.

History must be respected in a realistic historical novel, which means that the author must search out books and documents on which to base much of his work. This habit, too, can be transferred to the contemporary novel, as indeed seems to be the case in the abstract novels we have been considering. At least three of them are based on "sources." Galdós still leans rather heavily on other men's works.

Finally Galdós developed an idea of historical necessity, the inevitability of events presided over by Providence or Fate. The same notion, which is to figure prominently in later nonhistorical novels, already appears in *León Roch's Family*. Speaking of León's plan to submit his life to the control of reason, the author comments: "But men who dream of this grandiose victory do not count on the strength of what we might call *Social Fate*, an enormous and enslaving power" (887 - 88). The belief in historical necessity applied to contemporary events becomes determinism, a doctrine usually associated with Zola but which is already visible in Galdós's prenaturalistic novels. There is a definite carry-over from Galdós's historical novels to his early contemporary ones, a fact which heretofore seems to have passed unobserved.

CHAPTER 6

Mitigated Naturalism

I   Galdós's Conversion to Naturalism

DURING the period when Galdós was writing *León Roch's Family* he purchased six volumes of Zola's Rougon-Macquart series, all that had been published up to that time with one exception.[1] We have just noticed possible traces of the Frenchman's technique in the Spaniard's novel. Later in 1879 Galdós finished the Second Series of the *National Episodes* and in its epilogue he asserts that he will now devote himself to "contemporary types."[2] Yet the year 1880 passed with nothing new coming from his pen.

This blank year has various explanations.[3] One important factor was that Galdós spent the winter of 1879 - 80 and the following summer in Santander with his brother Ignacio and the latter's family. Ignacio was an army officer, who had lived for some years in Cuba and married a Cuban lady, and was now the military governor of Santander. Living with the family interrupted the regular routine of Galdós's production.

A second factor seems to have been disappointment in love. There is evidence that Don Benito greatly admired a young lady, Juanita Lund, the vivacious, well-educated daughter of a Norwegian Protestant merchant and a Basque mother. Galdós had met her in Santander three years before, when she was eighteen years old and he was thirty-one. He apparently put off declaring his love, waiting until she matured; but her marriage to Dr. Achúcaro on September 5, 1879, shocked him into a realization of his loss. It could also have contributed to the slackening of his productivity.

But a third, and perhaps the most important, cause of his inactivity was the study of Zola's methods and techniques. When his next novel, *La desheredada* (The Disinherited Woman), appeared it was immediately hailed as naturalistic. Clarín reviewed the first part[4] saying: "[this novel] has made me see very clearly that [Galdós] has

considered many of the doctrines of naturalism good and he has
written according to them and according to the example of the
naturalists." Another reviewer says that Galdós "makes use of Zola"
and that he "has read and studied Zola."[5] And although the Spanish
novelist himself minimized the influence of the chief of the
naturalistic movement, he did tell his friend Giner de los Ríos that in
The Disinherited Woman he wished "to enter a new path and to in-
augurate my *second* or *third manner,* as is said of painters."[6] The
study of Zola is undoubtedly one of the reasons why Don Benito laid
aside his pen during 1880.

There is no question that naturalism infuses Galdós's production
from 1881 — *The Disinherited Woman* — to 1889 — *Realidad*
(Reality) — and leaves traces even after the latter date. His first
novels in the new vein are more strictly naturalistic, although clearly
in a mitigated form. Later, beginning with *Fortunata and Jacinta,* an
element of spirituality becomes more and more prominent, until in
the 1890s it dominates his thought. It is the earlier naturalistic novels
that will concern us in this chapter.

First we must ask why Galdós, contrary to all other established
Spanish writers, threw in his lot with the young partisans of the new
school. Don Benito saw the latter as champions of liberalism, including freedom of thought, while the older men upheld
traditionalism in thought and idealism in fiction. The naturalists
proclaimed that the novel was to be a serious social study, based on
close observation of reality, presented with the objectivity of a scientist, discarding the imaginative fiction of idealism. To the extent
possible the laws of nature should determine the constitution and the
fate of its characters, and these laws worked through heredity and
environment. The protagonist is no longer the exceptional hero of
idealism but any man, because any man's life is a fit subject for a
novel. And since a story is seldom rounded out in real life, the concept of a "slice of life," a novel which begins and ends abruptly, had
some vogue. All these elements, or only a part of them, were
couched in a language which epitomized the cry for more liberty; in
this case the right to use words and portray situations which the
traditionalists labeled obscene.[7]

We shall see that these components of naturalism exist in Galdós's
novels, although in a less pronounced form than in those of French
authors. Don Benito never felt that he had to maintain a strictly ob-
jective point of view, concealing his opinions from the reader. He
does not hesitate to point a moral. He suggests obscenities by using

euphemisms but never employs the tabooed word. Another change from his previous works seems to be more of a reaction against, rather than an imitation of, Zola. The latter disdained and reviled the society of his times, but Galdós now drops the thesis novel with its polemics and satire and no longer chastises the Spanish world from the point of view of an outsider. He still has messages for his compatriots but now he includes himself in the group and finds himself subject to the national shortcomings. He understands sympathetically these foibles and presents them with a humor which reminds us more of Cervantes and of English writers than of the French.

In the last analysis Galdós's mitigated naturalism is a reconciliation of the traditional forms of the novel with Zola's school. The Krausistic philosophers believed that harmony could be reestablished between conflicting entities if each one realized that it was a subordinate part in a greater whole. Naturalism stressed the material fact, idealism the metaphysical origins of all reality. Galdós states clearly his belief that the particular fact is a manifestation of a higher law: hence philosophic thought and materialism, metaphysics and reality, are embraced in the same greater unit. "What one sees . . . is the least important part of what exists. All the big things, every law, every cause, every active element is invisible."[8] The "rational harmonizing" of the Krausists is basic to Galdós's mitigated naturalism.[9]

II   The Disinherited Woman (1881)

This novel recounts the decline and fall into prostitution of a young woman, Isidora Rufete. She is obsessed with the illusion of nobility, believing herself to be the illegitimate daughter of an aristocratic mother.

It is easy to pick out elements of naturalism in her portrayal. Her insane father encourages her in her obsession; her brother is an epileptic; her son is physically deformed. We see the hereditary infirmity taking different forms in three generations. Don Benito puts the family into a Cervantine frame by placing its origin in La Mancha and naming Isidora's uncle Santiago Quijano-Quijada; the uncle also encourages her delusion of grandeur. Environment becomes far more precise and realistic than in previous works. Every action is pinpointed in a known part of Madrid; yet the environment has little effect on the obsessed heroine[10] as long as her capacity to live in a dream world alienates her from her surroundings.[11] Only when her fall is complete and she has given up all pretensions to nobility does the coarseness of her environment bring her to gross language and vulgar manners (1148).

The historical moment, which constitutes part of the environment, is carefully fixed and skillfully used. Isidora takes her first step toward prostitution on the very evening when word of King Amadeo de Saboya's abdication is reaching the streets of Madrid. Just as he renounces his high noble title, so she relinquishes much of her claim to nobility. The second volume, whose action is two years later (in 1875), opens with a chapter which humorously mixes public and private events, intertwining the national destiny with that of the characters of the novel. Isidora is not the exceptional heroine; her misadventures are a kind of parody on the struggles of the heroine of romantic novels who, despite plenty of opportunities to attain ease and luxury at the price of her virtue, maintains her purity by plying her needle from dawn until midnight. In the contrast between real life and romantic imagination "realism parodies romance, and Don Quixote rides again."[12]

All these elements of naturalism, plus others which the reader will take on faith, exist in *The Disinherited Woman*. But on the other side of the ledger we must inscribe non-naturalistic factors — Galdós's humor, his subjectivism in speaking directly to the reader and commenting on the actions of his creatures, his avoidance of obscenities, and his pointing a moral at the end of the book.[13] Furthermore, underlying Isidora's fall is the idea Galdós expressed many times before — the destructive force of uncontrolled imagination, the loss of contact with reality. Isidora has a powerful imagination. Before events actually take place she previews them in her mind. "She had the custom of representing to herself in her imagination, very vividly, happenings before they were real."[14] Her inventions are like chapters out of a romantic novel. My situation is nothing new, she says. "Books are full of similar cases. I've read my own story so many times!" (972) Like a second Madame Bovary, Isidora creates a notion of what life should be from her reading of romantic novels.

Isidora's first step toward degradation occurs when she becomes the mistress of Joaquín Pez, a widower who had been married to a marchioness and is still, by courtesy, called a marquis. Of course, he is not truly a nobleman, but Isidora is dazzled by his title. For his sake she refuses offers of marriage from the young doctor Augusto Miquis, who continues to befriend her up to the last, and from Juan

Bou, a self-made owner of a printing establishment, proud of being one of the common people. She cannot bear the idea of degrading herself to their lowly level. Nonetheless when Joaquín loses all his money she is capable of selling herself to Bou and of attempting to seduce Miquis in order to support her lover. Joaquín goes to Cuba where he marries a rich woman. Isidora's liaisons involve her with men of progressively lower moral worth until her last lover is a shady gambler and criminal.

In the meantime her attempts to prove her relationship with the noble family have come to naught. She has taken her claim to the law courts but the documents on which she counted are fraudulent. She is jailed and is only released when she admits that she is not one of the noble family. With this admission, the delicacy which had been one of her traits — her love of cleanliness, the circumspection of her language — soon leave her and she becomes coarse and crude (1148). Rejecting the pleas of her old godfather José Relimpio, who sees her as a fairy princess to the last, she goes off to a house of prostitution.

Yet even while making her fall complete, the author cannot deny her some good traits. "In the loss of so many noble qualities she kept a little pity" (1153), and "she still was somewhat noble" (1154). Hence, although he would have us believe that Isidora disappears forever as her story ends, we are not really surprised to see her surface again in another novel as the compassionate mistress of a penniless artist, nursing him in a hopeless bout with tuberculosis.[15] Galdós seems to have found his original ending too harsh and he gives back to Isidora some very admirable qualities along with a new-found sense of reality.

The Disinherited Woman marks a great step forward in Galdós's art. It is a book full of admirable passages, skillfully drawn characters, marvelously observed and recorded descriptions. Limited space does not permit us to comment further on its many perfections.

III El amigo Manso *(Friend Manso, 1882)*

Máximo Manso is a professor of philosophy at the University of Madrid. He leads a very calm life, never departing from a routine of study, writing, and innocent recreation until his brother (José María) and family arrive from Cuba, which means that Máximo must give up his beloved habits to help find an apartment and install the family in it, to find a private tutor for the children, and even to

choose a wet nurse (with the help of Dr. Augusto Miquis) for the
newborn baby whose godfather he becomes.

For the post of tutor Manso remembers a young woman (Irene) he
had known from her childhood. Despite great difficulties she has
prepared herself in the Normal School for teaching. As the bachelor
Manso sees more and more of her in José María's house he comes to
believe her the embodiment of reason and his admiration turns to
idealistic love. His own timidity and fortuitous interruptions keep
him from declaring his love.

Meanwhile he has taken on Manolo Peña as a private student.
This young man, the son of Máximo's landlady, is extremely practical, the exact opposite of his teacher. He cries "I hate philosophy. I
can't make head or tail of metaphysics. . . . I like facts, life, specific
things. Don't speak to me of theories, speak of events; don't speak of
systems, speak of men" (O.C., IV, 1177). Finally Manso realizes that
Irene and Manolo are in love; bitterly disappointed for himself, he
humanely helps them overcome Manolo's mother's objection to their
marriage.

By this time Máximo sees that Irene was not the embodiment of
reason (la mujer razón) but rather a "womanly woman" (la mujer
mujer). He is surprised to discover that he loves her even more as a
real person, in spite of the faults natural to real beings. She has
ceased to be an abstraction; Manso's greater love for the real girl
parallels Galdós's renunciation of the abstract characters in his thesis
novels for the "real" individuals of his naturalistic works. Once Manso is disillusioned about Irene he knows that he had lost contact with
reality and that the good qualities he had imagined in her were projections from his own mind.

The action of the novel is fixed in the year 1880, precisely the year
that Galdós spent in Santander with brother Ignacio and his Cuban
family, the period in which his intention of proposing to Juanita
Lund was thwarted by her marriage, and the time in which his study
of Zola turned him away from the thesis novel to a new concept of
literary realism. In view of these similarities to Manso's life there is
little doubt that Don Benito himself was one of his models for Máximo. Galdós never modeled his major characters on a single original.
Several other models have been suggested and in all probability they
did contribute to the protagonist of Friend Manso.[16]

Manso, following Krausistic doctrine, extolls the preeminence of
the professional philosopher. "The philosopher discovers the truth
but he does not enjoy it. . . . The man of thought discovers the truth;

but the one who enjoys it and makes use of its celestial gifts is the man of action, the man of the world, who lives in specific events, in the contingencies and hubbub of everyday deeds" (1257). With these words Manso consoles himself for the loss of Irene, Galdós for the loss of Juanita Lund. The word *manso* can mean "meek, docile, lacking in virility" but it also signifies the "bellwether," the leader of the flock. Máximo (and Galdós?) has been *manso* in both senses.

Krausism always sought to harmonize conflicting aspects of a given subject. In literature the materialism of Zola threatened to submerge the idealistic school in oblivion. Máximo's reconciliation of opposed divisions of philosophy symbolizes Galdós's harmonization of literary theories in his mitigated naturalism.

The serious thought of *Friend Manso* is pretty well hidden for the casual reader. Don Benito presents his personages with sympathy and chides them humorously for their weaknesses. Manso himself is a Quixote and his world of philosophic speculation is as unreal as the visionary realm of the Knight of the Sad Countenance. In poking fun at these and other characters Galdós does not exclude himself. He knows that he, too, has been infected by the dreamworld virus.

Naturalism is not prominent in the work, although it can be seen especially in the subjection of various persons to natural laws. For example, when Manso finds out that Irene prefers young Manolo to himself, he tells her: "You are carrying out inescapably the law assigned to youth and beauty" (1266). All things considered, *Friend Manso* is one of Galdós's most delightful creations.

IV *Biographical Interlude*

At the same time that the author of *The Disinherited Woman* was bringing out this naturalistic work he was thinking of a scheme to gain further recognition and profit from his *National Episodes*. He proposed to issue an illustrated edition of the historical works, employing the best-known Spanish artists as well as contributing some sketches of his own. Apparently his friends warned him against risking a high-priced edition in an indifferent market, but Galdós was not to be deterred. The project proceeded slowly. Its epilogue carries the date "November, 1885."

The art work of the new edition received well-merited praise; nonetheless the publication was a financial disaster. In 1896, when Galdós and Cámara separated, the inventory showed several thousand unsold copies, mostly unbound and often in deteriorated or moldy condition.

The enthusiasm which Galdós provoked as the enemy of fanaticism in *Gloria* and *León Roch*[17] is evident in the reviews of the young men who were soon to exult over his conversion to naturalism. Two magazines which supported the naturalistic movement contain eulogistic articles on Galdós.[18] This adoration reached its apogee in the banquet which these youths planned and offered to their idol. Their gathering was dubbed "the Gall Club" owing to their witty and often bitter comments on the events of the day. At a dinner celebrating the staging of Eugenio Sellés's *Esculturas de carne* (Statues of Flesh), a mildly naturalistic play, either Sellés or Clarín — perhaps both — proposed the idea of a banquet for Galdós. Armando Palacio Valdés published an invitation to all who loved art and literature, not just the practitioners of the arts, to join in honoring a Spaniard who was bringing honor and glory to his country by his "incomparable genius and his amazing fecundity."[19] When the banquet was finally readied, on March 26, 1883, it was necessary to schedule it in two sections — a low-cost luncheon attended mainly by the impecunious young, and an elegant evening gathering where established authors, politicians, and public figures did homage to Don Benito.

The large gathering, about 230 persons, included not only the original naturalistic proponents, but men prominent in all walks of life. The honored guest, suffering apparently from one of his migraines, and certainly overwhelmed by timidity, escaped to Toledo but was pursued and brought back by some of his friends. He had written and caused to be printed a short expression of thanks before departing for Toledo; now, at the banquet, after hearing his praises from the great political leaders Cánovas del Castillo and Castelar, he asked a friend to read his printed reply. Many congratulatory telegrams from groups and individuals in other cities were read.

On the day following the banquet all the newspapers of Madrid, with the exception of those of Neo-Catholic leanings, gave it preferential coverage. *La Epoca* devoted almost all of its first page to it. A number of biographies of Galdós, filled with many inaccuracies and many, many encomiums, adorned the public press both before and after the banquet. All voices were raised in a chorus of praise.[20]

No doubt the young naturalists had hoped that the banquet would be a consecration of their literary beliefs. Perhaps they even hoped that Don Benito would speak in favor of the new school. If so, they were disappointed. The guest list, including names of men indifferent or opposed to naturalism, shows that the banquet became a tribute to the man, not a literary manifesto. Galdós never dreamed of becoming the leader of a faction. Because of his Krausistic desire to harmonize the conflicting literary postures Galdós was above the struggle.

V El Doctor Centeno *(1883)*

This two-volume novel, published in May and July not long after the banquet, is the beginning of a closely linked series that includes *Tormento* (Torment, March, 1884) and *La de Bringas* (The Bringas Woman, July, 1884). The linkage is brought about by the author's using the same characters, now in minor roles, now as protagonists, throughout the entire series. A large number of them are introduced in the first chapter of *Dr. Centeno,* which shows that he had the substance of the whole series in mind as he began the first volume. While it is true that other major characters — the Bringas family, Agustín Caballero, Jesús Delgado — are still waiting in the wings, we already have most of the individuals who play important roles in these novels.

These personages are by no means the first reappearing characters in Don Benito's work. He had to use, of course, many persons in more than one of his *National Episodes.* However, the return of Salomé Porreño and Bozmediano *(The Golden Fountain)* in *The Bold One (O.C.,* IV, 244, 318, 383, and 396), and the mention of Doña Perfecta and her brother Cayetano Polentinos in *León Roch's Family (O.C.,* IV, 806, 828, and 843) is a different matter, as there was no compelling need for the author to revive these characters from his earlier work. It is highly probable that he took this device from Balzac. Furthermore, the manner in which he integrates the novels of this new series is highly reminiscent of the *Comédie Humaine.*[21]

There are, in fact, a number of mentions of Balzac (1166, 1167, 1368, 1374, and 1384) in the second volume of *Dr. Centeno,* the action of which takes place in 1863 - 1864, when Benito was a university student just like the young men whose activities are recorded in this book. One of them, Arias Ortiz, "a great devotee of Balzac, had almost all his novels, and he knew the personages of the *Comédie Humaine* as if he had dealt with them personally." Galdós goes on to name nine principal Balzacian characters who "were as familiar to him as his friends" (1374). Since these scenes of student life are full of autobiographical reminiscences, the allusions to Balzac are another proof of the author's early admiration for the Frenchman.[22] Clearly Balzac was very much on Galdós's mind as he wrote *Dr. Centeno*, which justifies our statement that the device of a series of works integrated through repeated characters is mainly due to his influence.

Dr. Centeno deals with education — more with the lack of education than with any positive results of schooling. Felipe Centeno has come to Madrid with the noble desire to study and eventually to become a doctor. He is a penniless waif to whom Pedro Polo gives a job as household servant with the understanding that he may attend classes in the priest's school. Polo is himself only slightly ahead of his students. When he opened his school "he had to learn at night what he was to teach the following day . . . ; better said, Polo didn't teach anything."[23] Of course severe punishments are a fundamental part of such a program. The boredom and suffering of the boys is infinite. Felipe finds it almost impossible to commit to memory all the rote learning, although he does progress satisfactorily in reading. His treatment by Pedro Polo and by the latter's mother and sister becomes worse and worse. Even Ido del Sagrario, Polo's martyrized assistant, ridicules the waif.

Meanwhile the priest is falling in love with Amparo Sánchez Emperador, who comes occasionally to his house. Galdós reveals Polo's growing infatuation to us indirectly so we are not surprised, as Felipe is, when he sees the couple talking through the window grating one night. Polo begins to treat the lad better but at the first opportunity he dismisses him from his service.

After a fortnight in the slums Felipe finds Alejandro Miquis again at the observatory. Alejandro had been kind to him when they first saw each other there, and now he uses the boy as a messenger to his eccentric Aunt Isabel, from whom he expects a considerable sum of money. Felipe returns with the good news that the funds are available and Alejandro rewards him by taking him as his servant, or rather, his squire. For Felipe is to be a Sancho Panza to Alejandro's Quixote (1437).

The second volume, which is almost a separate and distinct work in itself, centers around Alejandro, his life in a student boarding house, his senseless generosity with his friends, his firm belief that his historical drama *El grande Osuna* (The Great Duke of Osuna) will be a sensational success, his unfortunate love affair with a grasping strumpet, and his impecunious suffering and death from tuberculosis. During Alejandro's last illness Felipe is reduced to begging in order to support his master, just as Lazarillo de Tormes supported the gentleman in Toledo.[24]

Alejandro, like Isidora Rufete, is from La Mancha, and dwells in a world of illusions (1357). Generous to a fault, he could not resist the requests of his friends, even when his purse was all but empty. He dies penniless, but like Don Quixote he has a last-minute realistic vision of his situation. He now abhors his mistress and wants his drama burned (1437 - 38). Disavowing his delusions he announces a new project, a play to be called *El condenado por confiado* (Condemned for Overconfidence)[25] which would be a realistic commentary on his own life.

The theme of education loses prominence in the second volume of *Dr. Centeno.* Felipe is sent to a secondary school for a while, and he finds that education there is reduced to learning Latin grammar. "And confused, full of doubts, he dared, in his ignorance, to protest against the badly taught and worse learned jargon, saying: 'I want them to teach me things, not this' " (1356). Again we see Spencer's shadow falling on Galdós.[26] Other suggestions from the English philosopher are visible in the ideas expressed by the strange madman Jesús Delgado, who had lost his job in the Office of Public Instruction (1376 - 77). So he retired to the boarding house where he passes his days and his nights writing letters to himself! The rascally students purloin a couple of them in which Delgado tells himself that he was born a century and a half too early(1378), recognizing that the opposition to his system of *Complete Education*[27] would eventually wither away. In the same letter he quotes phrases from Spencer's book. When the students, as a cruel but highly amusing practical joke, send Don Jesús a letter signed by the pet dog of the house (who rejoices in the name Julián of Capadocia) Delgado's answer is so appropriate that the boys cannot deny his keen intelligence (1381). It is a case of the Cervantine formula *la razón de la sinrazón* ("reason from unreason, or method in madness").[28] Neither Don Quixote nor Don Jesús Delgado can impose his visionary perfection on the "real" world, but that does not mean that his ideal is wrong.

So much for education *per se.* It may also be seen as a component of student life, which is the principal matter of the second volume. Alejandro Miquis's personal misadventures are scarcely typical, but the doings of his fellow students give a comprehensive and delightful picture of what Galdós himself must have observed in his first years in Madrid. Many passages of the book have an autobiographical ring.[29] Specifically, although Alejandro is definitely not a portrait of Don Benito, we can point out many actions and attitudes which they both share. Both hated the study of law (1368); both delighted in the novels of Balzac (1366) and in Hugo's *Les Misérables* (1400), which was published in 1862, just before the time at which the action of Galdós's novel takes place. Like the author, Alejandro loves to take long walks through the outskirts of the city (1369, 1385 - 86). Both buy many books (1372); both write plays and destroy their early dramas (1367); both are fond of the opera (1355 - 56). Alejandro is not especially fond of music other than the opera, but Arias Ortiz shares Benito's devotion and "prodigious musical memory" (1374).

Dr. Centeno hovers between the contemporary and the historical genre. The events depicted were twenty years in the past; Galdós twice invokes Clio, the muse of history (1302, 1305). Speaking of the unknown antecedents of Doña Virginia, the mistress of the boarding house, he says "All is darkness in that part of the nation's history . . . ," and calls on his memory asking it to help itself, if possible, with some historical document (1358). A certain humorous and fictionalized return to the methodology of the *National Episodes* is apparent.

Dr. Centeno is hardly a well-built novel. It is, however, a work of fascinating interest, more as a gallery of portraits and scenes rather than as a narrative of events. Contemporary critics complained of its plotlessness, something which seems due to its conception as a part of a series, in the manner of Balzac.

We have suggested the influence of Cervantes in the characters of Jesús Delgado and Alejandro Miquis. The author turns Cervantine humor against his own ideas as he ridicules his pompous Don Florencio defending *moderation* (1299) or Federico Ruiz trying to *harmonize* Science and Religion (1334). Alejandro's pathetic death scene is clearly modeled on Don Quixote's last hours and has much of the touching and moving quality of Cervantes's immortal passage.

VI   Tormento (*Torment, March, 1884*)

Dr. Centeno ended with a discussion of realism and idealism in a dialogue between José Ido del Sagrario and Felipe Centeno; *Torment* begins with another dialogue between the same interlocutors bearing on the same topic. Besides providing another obvious link between the two works, this conversation serves as an introduction to the underlying problem of the new novel: can orphan girls keep their innocence and virtue through interminable days of bleak needlework? Ido maintains the affirmative and is demonstrating his thesis by writing a romantic novel in which he takes his neighbors Amparo and Refugio Sánchez Emperador as models. He knows that their real life is not as austerely virtuous as represented in his "volcanic imagination"; yet he refuses to include these derogatory items "because they are not poetic." People would be scandalized if these prosaic things were put in a book (*O.C.*, IV, 1448).

But the realistic story which the idealist Ido del Sagrario deems unworthy of literature is precisely what Galdós is going to tell us. Satire of romantic idealism dominates the final chapters of *Torment*, where the author points out that in real life the rigors of virtue yield to seductive temptation and that an attempt to impose the patterns of idealistic literature results in ridiculous artificiality.

The love affair of Pedro Polo and Amparo surfaces in this work after having dropped out of sight throughout the second volume of *Dr. Centeno*. We learn that the priest had befriended the orphaned girls, paying for their father's funeral, and even selling some of his clothes to provide them with food (1490). Galdós makes it clear that Amparo gave in to the priest's advances, she is now tormented by remorse and has completely broken off the relationship. Polo in his turn calls her his "torment"; his continuing infatuation has brought out the harsh irascibility of his nature and caused him to lose his chaplaincy, his school, and finally his license to say mass (1484, 1486). He dreams of going far away, of escaping to the Philippine Islands with Amparo, there to begin a new existence (1489, 1491). Abandoned by all save Father Nones, an old, truly charitable priest, he is sent to a country estate to recuperate physically before being packed off to the Philippines — without his "Torment" and still active in his priestly role.

But while Polo is falling into ruin Amparo's fortunes are rising. She has been helping in the household of the Bringas family, where, as a distant relative, her position lies in the nebulous area between a friend and a servant. Rosalía Pipaón de la Barca de Bringas, the wife, is a pretentious snob, very demanding in the tasks imposed on Amparo and sarcastically mordant in her criticism of the young woman (1455, 1511). Amparo, modest, timid, and above all weak-willed, submits to this treatment while Refugio, much more spirited and rebellious, asserts her independence.

In the Bringas household Amparo meets Agustín Caballero, a man in his forties who has recently returned from Mexico and

Brownsville, Texas. By struggling in mining camps and later by supplying armies during the American Civil War he has gained a fortune and now wants to return to civilization and shake off the crudities of his former life (1457 - 59, 1468). He hopes to marry, although he is not attracted to most Spanish girls, who strike him as presumptuous and flighty (1469). He soon finds his ideal in Amparo, but his excessive timidity makes it almost impossible for him to propose (1467).

When he finally declares himself Amparo's real torment begins. She feels she would be deceiving Agustín if she did not confess her liaison with Pedro Polo to him. The priest complicates her situation by forcing her to visit him under threat of some violent action. Amparo is so weak-willed and undecided that she simply cannot take a stand. So she drifts along, in an agony of indecision, knowing that word of her past will almost surely reach her fiancé from those who know about it. Suicide seems to be her only escape.

In the splendidly furnished house which Agustín has prepared for her Amparo resolves to take the fatal step. She sends Felipe Centeno, who has become one of Caballero's servants, to buy poison. She writes a brief note "All is true. I am not worthy of pardon, but rather pity"; she swallows the "poison," which is really a toothache remedy, which Felipe has substituted for the deadly formula. Its strong alcoholic content clouds her vision and brings on a dull stupor, not without her experiencing the emotions of "dying" and recognizing the similarity of her action to episodes of romantic novels and plays (1544, 1550). Of course the false suicide is nothing but a parody on the romantic idealism of popular subliterary novels.

Realism now takes over. Caballero has planned a wedding trip to Bordeaux. At the last moment he decides to take Amparo with him but not as his wife. Francisco Bringas is at the station to see Agustín off and is surprised to find that Caballero is not alone. Furthermore the two "guilty" parties are not shamefaced and furtive; in fact they are supremely happy (1557). Bringas reports his observations to his wife, claiming an offended morality he did not show at the station, and Rosalía expresses indignation which ill becomes a woman soon to become truly immoral in Galdós's next novel.

If the novel is a parody of romantic idealism, as was hinted in the opening dialogue, it is also a social criticism. For example, the pettiness of the Bringas family and of society in general is symbolized in Don Francisco's interpretation of the loss of his new overcoat, which was stolen from the cloakroom of the royal palace. In this deed

Bringas sees the coming of the revolution![30] Part of the criticism of Spanish society comes from Agustín Caballero. He writes to his cousin: "The young people of this land drive me to drink. These girls — the poorer they are, the more haughty. Their education is nonexistent" (1503). Caballero sees Madrid with virgin eyes. Coming from the wilds of the New World, expecting to find a perfect society, he encounters pretense and false values. Thus he is part of a literary tradition, best known in Montesquieu's *Persian Letters,* where criticism of the supposed perfections of European civilization is voiced by men from a far-off and "inferior" culture. Spanish literature offers the same device in Baltasar Gracián's *El Criticón* (1651 - 57), in Cadalso's *Cartas marruecas* (1793), and in Espronceda's *El diablo mundo* (1841).

Agustín is, then, the outsider who finds fault with the establishment just as the youthful Benito excoriated aspects of peninsular society when he came from the relatively backward Canary Islands. There is certainly no one-to-one correspondence between Benito and Agustín; yet there are ways in which the latter resembles the former. He is "passionately fond of children" (1460); he speaks in so low a voice that he must often repeat his words (1505); his timidity is so great that he can hardly bring himself to propose marriage to Amparo.

Agustín has yet another criterion by which to judge the shortcomings of Madrid life. He has been in London, where Galdós had spent a month in the previous summer of 1883, and the contrast between English and Spanish ways works in favor of the former. When Caballero furnishes his house it is done "giving heed more to comfortable arrangement, according to English usage, than to that luxury of Latin people who sacrifice their own well-being to vain appearances" (1502). What astounds the Spanish ladies is the kitchen stove, "a huge iron contraption, of genuine English construction," which only lacked wheels to be a locomotive (1522). And even Agustín and Amparo's love was not in the Spanish mold "which has in its very intensity the germ of its short duration; it was love English-style, deep, sure and unswerving, firmly seated on a foundation of domestic ideas" (1516). Agustín is not alone in his criticism of Spanish society. Galdós, speaking directly to the reader, deplores as before the low quality of education (1462). Above all he condemns living above one's means, a Spanish trait as universal at the time *Torment* was being written as it was when the fictitious action took place (1464).

We have already given brief indications of the character of Amparo, Pedro Polo, and Rosalía Bringas. We must say a few words about Francisco Bringas. Like Isidora Rufete and the Miquis brothers he is from La Mancha. He considers himself important to the government, although he occupies a bureaucratic position where little real work is done. His passion is thrift. Every expense of the household has a corresponding item in his budget. A kind man, as shown in his aid to Amparo, he falls short of real goodness through keeping his own selfish interest ever uppermost in his mind. Galdós ironically dubs him "our good Thiers," equating him with the French statesman who, in his writings on economics, glorifed work and property.[31] In addition, the author counted on his readers' familiarity with Thiers's photograph often reproduced in the illustrated magazines. "A happy coincidence relieves us from drawing his portrait, since two words are sufficient. . . . He was the exact image of Thiers" (1450).

The theme of dreams versus reality (or idealism versus history) is clearly stated when Agustín meditates on the manner in which the hopes he had brought to Spain have been defeated. He wanted a regular, well-ordered life, a virtuous wife and family. But circumstances have willed otherwise. He tells himself, "Don't call it lawlessness, but rather law; because life imposes it on you, and we don't make life, but life makes us. . . . Don't trust the conventional majesty of principles but [on the contrary] kneel before the resplendent altar of facts. . . . If this is folly, so be it" (1556). Principles are a kind of idealism, a series of rules of conduct which we want to impose upon life. Just as literary idealism creates its unreal world, so moral principles lead to unreality. The factual world can intercede, the inevitable course of history can destroy our dream world.

VI   La de Bringas (*The Bringas Woman, July, 1884*)

In Torment we saw all Madrid society living beyond its means and pretending to a high status unjustified in reality. This theme was secondary in *Torment* but becomes the dominant motif in *The Bringas Woman.*[32]

Status can, of course, be based on the wide recognition of real worth achieved through positive contributions in art, learning, social betterment, altruistic or virtuous acts. This is not what concerns Galdós; it is, rather, the appearance of status, specifically as given by associating with persons of the aristocracy, by summering with the elite on the beaches of the north, by disdaining everyone of lower position, and by dressing in the latest styles. His heroine, Rosalía de Bringas, uses all these means of giving herself an air of social importance. Her passion for clothes embroils her in financial deceit and finally in sexual immorality, so that ultimately she is quite frankly willing to sell her body for the means of maintaining the appearance of status.

Running parallel with the story of Rosalía's complicated deceits and her pretense is the situation of Queen Isabel II. During the action time of the novel, from February to September, 1868, discontent with the queen and her government was mounting even higher, to culminate in the "glorious revolution," which deposed Isabel from the throne. The parallels between events in the Bringas family and the royal one are obvious. Both live in the Royal Palace, the queen in her sumptuous rooms, Rosalía in one of the numerous apartments of the upper floors, a maze of passageways, rooms, and terraces where employees of the palace and recipients of the queen's favor lived isolated from Madrid in a little city of their own.[33] Francisco Bringas does not have to step outside of the enormous building in order to go to his office (1659); his isolation and later on his blindness correspond to the lack of contact with national realities on the part of the queen and her government. The fall of Queen Isabel corresponds to Rosalía's fall from conjugal virtue, and the collapse of the royal government, to Francisco Bringas's loss of control over family direction and finances.

Don Francisco makes a veritable religion out of careful planning, even to such details as the dishes served at the family's meals (1600, 1624). An unforeseen outlay is to be avoided like the plague. His closefisted economy conflicts with the essential element in his wife's desire for ostentation, for free spending is at the heart of achieving the appearance of status. When he condemns the family to spend the summer in the scorching heat of Madrid, and when he refuses the governorship of a province in order to continue in his tranquil and unpretentious position in the royal household (1586), he stimulates a spirit of rebellion in his wife.

Rosalía can yearn for the various things her husband denies her, but the only way she can rebel against his stinginess is by deceiving him in the matter of her wardrobe. Her passion for clothes becomes a dominant trait when Agustín Caballero cedes to her all the finery he had bought for his projected wedding with Amparo. She becomes friendly with Milagros, the Marquesa de Tellería (see *León Roch's Family*), whom she admires first as a person of title and second as a supreme authority in styles. The Marquesa also leads her into the labyrinth of deceit by urging her to buy a cloak and charge it on account (1578). To explain the new acquisition Rosalía says it was a gift of the queen, but when the bill comes due she is forced to borrow money unbeknown to her husband. But she only pays half of her bill, lending part of the rest to Milagros and buying even more material for a dress (1580). Thus begins a whole series of deceptions, greatly aggravated when Francisco's temporary blindness allows her to obtain the key to the strongbox in which Bringas keeps his savings.

During this time Don Manuel Pez (father of Joaquín Pez who figured in *The Disinherited Woman*) is a constant visitor in the Bringas household and he and Rosalía find good reasons to sympathize with one another. Pez's wife has become a religious fanatic, under the influence of Serafinita Lantigua (see *Gloria*). He complains of her lack of affection. Rosalía, on her part, voices her grievances against her husband's parsimony. Gradually the two begin to feel an attraction which could lead to adultery. Although Rosalía is sure that she would be much happier with Pez than with Bringas she rejects Pez's first attempt to seduce her (1627) and feels quite vain on two scores: her virtue and her ability to inspire passion (1628). But she now is sure that Pez will come to her rescue if, as they eventually do, her financial manipulations reach a point impossible of solution. Great is her disillusion when she does give herself to him and gets nothing in return!

Galdós makes a subtle analysis of his unattractive heroine's psyche. She vacillates in her affection for her husband, feeling love for him when he suffers and after her infidelity (1643), but as his health improves and his sight returns her regard for him diminishes (1621). His stinginess causes ideas of woman's liberation to germinate in her mind. She rationalizes that her deceits were necessary to show "that she had ceased to be a slave and that she assumed her portion of sovereignty in the distribution of the conjugal fortune. . . . She who had been a slave for so long, why shouldn't she do as she pleased occasionally? Every one of those fraudulent and clandestine actions delighted her before and after it was done" (1619, 1630). So she develops a code based on the axiom that "Necessity is what forms character" (1638), and she concludes that her sins are simply the natural result of her necessities (1642 - 43).

The grand finale comes when Rosalía, having lost all hope of help from Pez and obliged to repay the money lender Torquemada in three hours under threat of having the latter reveal all her duplicity to her husband, seeks a loan from Refugio Sánchez Emperador. She is tremendously humiliated by having to seek Refugio's aid, and this young woman takes sweet revenge on the haughty suppliant, alternately raising her hopes of getting the money and then dashing them, playing with her like a cat with a ball of paper (1650). Just before the climactic hour at which Rosalía must pay Torquemada, Refugio lectures Rosalía on Milagros's false friendship. The supreme blow is when she reveals that the Marquesa has called Rosalía *cursi* ("common, a fake"). But she does lend the money, and Torquemada receives it in the nick of time.

So Rosalía is saved, the revolution takes place, Bringas's world is shattered, and he becomes childlike (1618). Rosalía assumes the headship of the family, which she will support by seducing men of wealth. In the last lines of the novel the narrator implies that she made an unsuccessful attempt to make him one of her victims (1657).

Not just Rosalía, but the whole society of the time, is depicted as a sham. Everyone is living on borrowed money and no one pays his debts. Refugio tried to establish a business in women's clothing but had to give it up because no one paid her (1646). Milagros, supposedly a representative of the cream of society, lives from hand to mouth, and borrows not only from Rosalía but also from Refugio. Aristocratic women think nothing of smuggling clothes in from France. All of the upper class is rotten.

In contrast Galdós admires the conduct of the common people at the time of the revolution. Although Bringas is certain that there will be violent excesses, the militia that guards the palace even suffers hunger rather than steal food (1655). No harm is done by the masses; unfortunately it is not they, but politicians of the stripe of Pez, who control the new government (1656).

Finally, a few words about naturalism in this novel. The relative plotlessness of the novel recalls the "slice of life" technique. Obviously Rosalía's credo that "Necessity forms character" is a sort of determinism. The Bringas children have personalities like their parents — Alfonso like his mother and Isabel like her father (1637) — a clear case of heredity. But above all naturalism appears in the sordid pretense of Madrid society where the poor dress as if they were rich and dress is the façade which hides the rotten interior.

VII   Lo prohibido (*Forbidden Fruit, 1885*)

With this new novel Galdós introduced a different cast of characters and dropped the scheme of interlocking novels he had been pursuing for the past two years. While it is true that some of the characters of previous novels reappear in minor roles, the protagonists of *Forbidden Fruit*, all members of the Bueno de Guzmán family, do not appear in any earlier work.

But if Don Benito abandons the actors of his last creations he does not renounce the theme of these works. *Forbidden Fruit* merely turns to a higher class of society to show that the same striving for status, the same living beyond one's means, and the same moral corruption exist in the high bourgeoisie as in the petty bourgeois class. A craving for luxury with which to dazzle her friends leads to the degradation of the principal female character, Eloísa, just as it did in the case of Rosalía Bringas. Galdós, however, introduces another element, a commonsense, financially stable attitude that he identifies with the English way of life and incarnates to a degree in two of his characters.

José María Bueno de Guzmán is the son of a frivolous Andalusian playboy (*O.C.*, IV, 1689) and an English mother. He was educated in England where morality was stressed (1689a). As his relations with his cousin Eloísa develop, he yields now to the Andalusian, now to the English side of his heredity (1699b). "From my mother I got a certain spirit of rectitude, ideas of order; from my father, fragility, . . .[and an] enthusiasm for skirts" (1761b). He does not have strength to choose and direct his life; on the contrary he drifts with whatever current is pushing him. Clearly he is a naturalistic character, not a "hero" like those of earlier idealistic novels (1761a).

To emphasize the naturalistic element Galdós has devised a family (the Bueno de Guzmáns) in which common heredity has produced a variety of physical and mental disorders. José María suffers from periods of depression with a pathological fear of the unknown (1663a), often accompanied by an annoying buzzing in his ears.[34] When, at the age of thirty-six, he comes to establish himself in Madrid, after a successful business career in southern Spain, he gets to know for the first time his uncle Rafael and the latter's family. Don Rafael tells José María about the family flaw and how it manifests itself like a "chemical agent" (1665b) in the various members of the group. The uncle himself has the sensation of being suspended in the air and a fear of falling (1665a). His brother Serafín is a kleptomaniac (1664b). Three of his four children suffer as follows: Raimundo has spells of stammering (1677); María Juana feels she gets something like cloth between her teeth which she must chew and swallow (1665b - 1666a); Eloísa has a morbid fear of feathers, the sight or mention of which starts a tickling in her throat

(1666a). Only the youngest daughter, Camila, has escaped some physical symptom of the family trouble, but her volatile, madcap nature makes some people fear that she will end up in an insane asylum (1666b).[35] José María finds her almost repugnant when he first meets her (1669b), but in a few years he becomes enchanted with her spontaneous, natural ways, full of *joie de vivre*.

These manifestations of heredity give a strongly naturalistic color to *Forbidden Fruit*. We can add a few details. The medical element is important, partly in the use of medical terminology and partly in the manner of describing infirmities and death. When Carrillo (Eloísa's husband) dies, "his shouts were the exclaiming of a wounded and endangered animal, without thought, with nothing to distinguish the man from the beast" (1741b). Eloísa herself is terribly disfigured by a malady which bloats her face to the extent that "it was necessary to have recourse to the most ugly zoological species to find something resembling her" (1813b).

Toward the end of the book José María suffers a stroke with resulting paralysis, again described in a naturalistic manner (1860b - 1863b). Since he is the presumptive author of the novel (his memoirs) he is forced to hire an amanuensis to finish it. He chooses our old aquaintance José Ido del Sagrario (from *Dr. Centeno* and *Tormento*), who would like to romanticize his employer's misadventures. But the latter will not permit fiction to alter reality, being unwilling "to contravene the law that I imposed upon myself from the beginning, and it was to tell in plain language my prosaic adventures in Madrid from the autumn of '80 to the summer of '84, events which are not at all different from those which fill and constitute the life of other men, and not to aspire to produce more effects than those which the simple and sincere stating of the truth produces, without the intent of moving the spirit of the reader with recherché terrors, surprises, and tricks of thought and of phrase, making things appear one way and then [having them] turn out otherwise" (1873b - 1874a). These words are practically a manifesto of Galdós's concept of naturalism. But, important as naturalism is, it does not overshadow the theme of social pretense, although this, too, is presented from the same naturalistic point of view.

The slow-moving action of the story concerns José María's relations with his three cousins, Eloísa, María Juana, and Camila. They are all married, but this only makes them more interesting to him, for, as he says, "I only like forbidden things, those which I shouldn't have" (1795a). His principal affair is with Eloísa, and it is one in which her ostentatious luxury makes deep inroads into José María's prosperity. When Eloísa's husband, Pepe Carrillo, inherits a large house and a modest fortune, she soon fills the house with extravagant *objets d'art* (1693a). José María overwhelms her with gifts (1702a) and, during a stay in Paris with her, satisfies her desire for jewelry and clothes, so that by the end of the summer he has spent all of his income for the year (1703b). When English common sense again predominates he finds his fortune diminished by ninety thousand dollars (1704a) and that Carrillo's assets are also near the point of exhaustion (1704b - 1705a). But Eloísa, determined to make a great display, inaugurates a series of Thursday dinners and receptions, the height of pretense, in which all thought of economy is thrown to the winds. José María soon realized that the Thursdays were "a cold cult of vanity. . . . All was wind, smoke, and the sterile satisfaction of having people talk about her house and her way of life" (1721a). So Eloísa has to borrow from Torquemada (1728a), and José María has to come to her financial rescue (1730, 1750b).

While all this is going on Pepe Carrillo is coming closer and closer to death. He is an idealistic man, who wants to improve Spain and who takes the English aristocracy and government as his models (1699b). But like his wife he, too, is a spendthrift. He endows a political newspaper to propagate his English ideal (1705a), gives to charities, and founds an orphan asylum (1726b). He is a kind of lay-saint (1727b, 1743b) with the incompetence in practical affairs one expects of a saint.

After Carrillo's death Eloísa becomes less and less attractive to José María (1748b - 1749b). He tries, as he has before, to get her to trim her extravagant spending. She pretends to take his advice but afterward does whatever she pleases (1750b). So they soon quarrel (1757, 1759b) and José María rejects her idea of a marriage between them (1757b). Eloísa continues her showy way of life, financed by a series of lovers — the Marqués de Fúcar, the Marqués de Flandes, the hateful Sánchez Botín — and suffers the alternatives of opulence and poverty.

A factor which stimulates his hatred of Eloísa is his growing love for Camila, the cousin he had considered repugnant on first knowing her. He comes to see that her natural spontaneity is a virtue, and that her love for her husband Constantino Miquis (brother of Augusto and Alejandro) is unshakable, no matter what he does to try to seduce her. As she says: "We love each other like Adam and Eve" (1782a). Because of his constant attentions (1836b) everyone believes that José María has had his way with her. Constantino wants a duel (1842a) and refuses José María admittance to his house (1860a). At this time the latter suffers his stroke, is nursed by the compassionate young couple (Camila and Constantino), and develops a purely idealistic love for them both. He leaves them what little money remains to him after a stock-market crash (1853b - 1856). They have now lost their pristine innocence and have been expelled from Eden (1846b, 1850a), but they will face down gossip.

In passing we should note that Camila and Constantino live within their very limited means, something which can be said of only one or two other characters of the novel. Clearly this happily married pair represents Galdós's ideal, in sharp contrast to the other couples he depicts and to the irregular affairs of his protagonist. The essence of their happiness is their profound mutual love, shaken once or twice by doubt and jealousy, but triumphant in the long run. Camila has none of the hereditary weaknesses of the family simply because she has no frustrations. Undoubtedly her lack of sexual frustration contributes to her good health. José María thinks that if he could marry her "all my nervous maladies, whether coming from the family diathesis or not, would leave me" (1829b). Similarly, María Juana's affliction has affected her only rarely since her marriage (1666a).

We must now glance briefly at José María's relations with his third cousin. María Juana has a small role in the novel, but she is an interesting psychological type. Because she presumes to be a learned woman, she reads the modern French and Italian authors as well as English writers in translation (1793b). She also presumes to give José María advice on the conduct of his life and love affairs, especially by trying to arrange a marriage for him (1794b - 1795a). With all her strength of mind she is not above imitating her sisters. Like Eloísa she has dinners and receptions; later, she tries "to assimilate as much as possible the forms of Camila's most singular character" (1846b), hoping to win José María away from his love for her. For in her intellectual way she seduces her cousin, telling him "not without using pretty circumlocutions and paraphrases, that the beneficial treatment that Madame Warens used with Jean Jacques to keep him from vice should be applied to me" (1831a).[36] José María finds this relationship odious shortly after its beginning and cannot understand the subtlety of loving him in order to save him from love (1831).

María Juana projects herself into these roles as a reaction against her drab existence, subjected to her husband's methodical economic stability. Cristóbal Medina has all the virtues of a good business man. He spends only one third of his income (1797a) and life with him is dull. He is a second Don Francisco de Bringas, capable of restricted generosity (1804a), but never dropping his prudence in a burst of openhanded liberality. María Juana, despite her intellectualism, seeks the unexpected, the unordered, in short, the romantic.

Her imagination is not nearly so powerful as that of other members of the Bueno de Guzmán family. Her brother Raimundo is a dreamer, suffering from an excess of imagination (1665b, 1684a). Eloísa is both tormented and consoled by her illusions. She says, "I am like my brother, who goes to bed thinking he is the prime minister and winds up believing it. . . . I go to bed thinking I am Mrs. Rothschild" (1693a). José María finds Raimundo's imaginative living contagious, and he proceeds to delude himself into believing that Eloísa is his wife (1685a), and later to forge romantic fictions about himself and Camila (1833a).

Since most of the Bueno de Guzmáns dream of felicities attainable only with money, their physical ills are often brought on by its lack. In many cases an attack of their nervous disease is cured simply by receiving money from José María (1737a, 1767b, 1773a). A purely materialistic weakness (loss of money) is linked to a psychological infirmity, a mental cast which produces physical disorders.

Of course work could be the remedy for financial insecurity and its resulting mental and physical disturbances. In fact José María does work for a time and finds it acts as a medicine to reestablish his health (1790). Cristóbal Medina, the worker who is a foil to his wife's family, never has psychosomatic troubles. But Galdós, using Raimundo as his spokesman, declares that Spaniards in general, "living in a world of phantoms, the perverse creations of chivalry and false sanctity" have lost their industry and do not work (1717b - 1718a). They want the comfort and luxury they see in other nations but justify their indolence on the religious grounds that one should not covet the things of this world. So without working they try to live in luxury that is beyond their means. It becomes a game of hiding financial ruin and bad debts (1667b). Don Rafael calls the lust for luxury "the Madrid evil" which brings on a deplorable tolerance of "infractions of the law, both moral and economic" (1851b).

In *Forbidden Fruit* the author has combined two of his constant preoccupations: the positive value of work and the negative force of uncontrolled imagination. English attitudes toward work and restraint of fantasy could correct the Spanish weakness, but in this novel they are not powerful enough to overcome Carrillo's and José María's Spanish nature.

Critical reaction to *Forbidden Fruit*, as well as to the novels which immediately preceded it, was on the whole unfavorable. Clarín did his best to stem the tide.[37] Ortega Munilla, another of Galdós's staunch friends, tempered his praise with adverse criticism, deploring the leisurely pace of the narrative and the excessive detail of the analysis of social evils.[38] Another critic censured the lack of plot and the insistence on abnormal psychology.[39] The modern reader finds much interest in details of the work but relatively little to praise in the book as a whole, especially when he compares it with novels Don Benito wrote in the next few years.

CHAPTER 7

Spiritual Naturalism:
The Beginnings

I A New Orientation

AS we just saw, the novels of Galdós's period of mitigated naturalism were progressively losing public and critical acceptance. By the time *Forbidden Fruit* appeared even those who favored naturalism qualified their praise with fault-finding reservations. Nor did the Spanish reading public — very limited in number — buy these books with the enthusiasm they showed for the *National Episodes* and the earlier thesis novels.

There followed a period of two years in which Galdós published nothing. Then came *Fortunata and Jacinta*. We must enter into details concerning the dates of the composition and publication of this masterpiece, for the delay in its appearance has a significance to be unearthed. In his *Memoirs* Galdós tells us that he began to write it "with elements gathered before" as soon as he returned from a trip to Portugal in the summer of 1885 (*O.C.*, VI, 1736). Following his custom of putting the date at the end of his manuscripts he placed "January 1886" on the last page of the first volume of his four-volume *magnum opus*. But this does not mean that he gave the manuscript to the printer at that time.

Finally, on April 18, 1887, Ortega Munilla announced the publication: "The literary news of the week is the appearance of a novel by Pérez Galdós."[1] Soon afterward (April 25, 1887) Ortega reviewed not just volume I of *Fortunata and Jacinta* but the first and second tomes which came out practically simultaneously. He begins by noting that "for two long years the master Galdós hadn't added a title to the long and glorious list of his novels." His statement refers to the fact that volume I of *Forbidden Fruit* (Galdós's last novel) was published in mid-April, 1885, and that the second part appeared early in May.[2] We must try to account for such a long gap in Don Benito's productivity.

Certainly he did not cease writing because he found himself in an affluent financial position. With his brother Ignacio he was in the midst of paying off the debts left by their deceased brother Domingo. But the long drawn-out publication of the illustrated *National Episodes* was finally completed,[3] at which time he could hope for an increase in their sale. We have already seen that the public did not respond and that the enterprise turned out to be a disappointment.

One reason for Galdós's lack of production may have been his entrance into politics. In those days all elections were rigged. The government in power could easily make its candidate the victor by finding some "irregularity" in the ballots cast for his opponent. By this process Galdós was "elected" for the district of Guayama in Puerto Rico.[4]

We can hardly fail to be astounded at this immorality and political chicanery and at Don Benito's willingness to accept its results, but of course we are judging the affair from a point of view which did not prevail at the time of the occurrence. Some of Galdós's friends were dismayed because they thought that politics would take him away from literature, not because of the manner in which he was made a deputy.[5] Galdós justifies his acceptance as follows: "Don't grieve about my being a deputy. I am not and never will be a politician. I've gone to Congress because they took me there, and I didn't resist because for a long time I've wanted to know political life at first hand. Now [that I am] in the Congress, I'm happier every day for having yielded, because without mixing in any aspect of active politics, I'm coming to understand that it is absolutely impossible to know national life without having gone through that building. How much one learns! What one sees! What a school!"[6] Galdós was not remiss in attending the sessions of the legislative body, and he recalls with pleasure the many friends he made among the deputies (*O.C.*, VI, 1738). But he did almost nothing to improve national well-being or to favor the interests of his district in far-off Puerto Rico. On the positive side, we must remember that Galdós was voting for the Liberal party and, when first in the Congress, he believed in the plans of Sagasta, its leader.

Politicians in his novels do not evoke his sympathy. It is curious to note that José María Bueno de Guzmán (in *Forbidden Fruit*) had also been made a deputy and had ignored his political duties. Don Benito viewed this inactivity with disapproval (*O.C.*, IV, 1678, 1707, and 1769). Another Galdosian character, Angel Guerra, is completely disillusioned after serving in the Congress. He sees no chance of national regeneration through politics, reflecting the feelings of the author who began to write the novel *Angel Guerra* (1890 - 91) less than a year after he ceased to be a deputy.

Other factors are more important as an explanation of the long delay in the appearance of *Fortunata and Jacinta*. First, Galdós felt that he wanted both volumes I and II to be read without a long time gap between them. In letters to his friends he urges them to go on to volume II without delay, for he feels that the first volume is weaker and will not, taken alone, give the right impression to the reader.[7]

But the most decisive reason for his delay was undoubtedly his discovery of a new kind of naturalism in Russian literature, particularly in Tolstoy's *War and Peace*. Just as his discovery of Zola brought on a year of no production (1880), a year given over in large part to study and reorientation, so Russian influences caused him to pause and meditate on the direction his new work would take. We should note that almost all critics have been aware of this fundamental change in Galdós's literary thought. As early as 1897, when Don Benito entered the Academy, the outstanding critic Menéndez y Pelayo spoke of *Fortunata and Jacinta* as a genial work "which initiates a change in [Galdós's] predilections and way [of writing]."[8]

There were any number of things which would draw the Spaniard's attention to Russia, so many, in fact, that we shall only be able to mention a few of them. News articles, especially concerning the nihilists' attempts on the life of the Tzar and their final success in assassinating him (1881), filled Spanish newspapers. The influential *Revue des Deux Mondes* (which Galdós almost surely read in the Atheneum) printed many articles on Russian politics, accounts of travels in Russia, and studies of Russian literature during the years which preceded *Fortunata and Jacinta*. There is every reason to believe that Galdós, whose career as a journalist left him attuned to current happenings, was aware of Russian events. Indeed, in 1884, shortly after Turgenev's death, when interviewed by the Russian I. Pavlovskii, he declared that the late author "was my great teacher."[9] Even more important is a letter from the same interviewer who asks Don Benito, "Have you received the novel of Tolstoi, which they sent you from Paris at my request?"[10] This letter, dated Feb. 4, 1885, shows that *War and Peace* reached Galdós before he began the composition of *Fortunata and Jacinta*.[11]

Galdós makes no public acknowledgment of his interest in Tolstoy until after much of his great novel was written. When Emilia Pardo Bazán lectured on *The Revolution and the Novel in Russia* Don Benito called it "the literary event of the day" and added "in the last few years the Russian novelists Tolstoy and Dostoievsky, both so original, have become popular in Paris. They captivate the French public perhaps even more than the indigenous and celebrated masters Zola and Daudet."[12] Again a couple of months later he mentions Tolstoy, Turgenev, and Dostoevski.[13]

Galdós did read *War and Peace*[14] and marked many passages by turning down or turning up a corner of the page. Unfortunately for us this does not permit us to know exactly what passage on a marked page interested him. Volume III particularly elicited his attention. In it Don Benito turned down twenty-one pages.

Now our problem is first, what did Galdós find in *War and Peace?* And secondly, is it correct to conclude that the impact of Tolstoy's novel was so great that it caused Galdós to reorient his ideas on naturalism? Unfortunately, he never made a statement about Tolstoy which would serve to answer these questions for us. We shall search out similarities between the two novels in a moment, but first let us hear what another intelligent Spaniard, Emilia Pardo Bazán, had to say about Russian naturalism. Quoting Vogüé (*Le Roman russe*, on which she leans far more than she admits) Doña Emilia says that French realists "are unaware of the best part of humanity which is the spirit." She adds that "this is really so, and for some time I have been thinking and writing that realism, to carry out fully its program, must include matter and spirit, earth and heaven, the human and the superhuman. I agree completely with Vogüé when he believes that naturalism . . . ought not close its eyes to the mystery which lies beyond rational explanations." The Russians do not fall into this error. "The spiritual element of the Russian novel is for me one of its most singular merits."[15] We can, I think, assume that Don Benito's reaction to Russian naturalism, and specifically to *War and Peace*, was much like that of his contemporary.

Tolstoy constantly makes the point that men are not free from historical determinism. On a page turned up in Galdós's copy he states that the French invasion happened not because Napoleon willed it, but "because it was bound to come to pass," following natural, historical laws which are only partly known. Galdós had come to similar thoughts on history even before his acquaintance with Tolstoy (see p. 62).

So in *War and Peace* there is a kind of narrowly deterministic naturalism (the war had to happen, p. 565; Moscow had to be burned, p. 838)[16] against which is opposed spiritual force manifest in the spirit of the army (pp. 754 and 963); in love (pp. 884 and 1050); and in Nature (pp. 256, 266, 356 - 57, and 943). Pierre discovers the force of the spirit in the person of Platon Karataev, the primitive, unspoiled man of the people, the peasant who loved everyone and yet no one (p. 905). "Every word and every action of his was the expression of a force uncomprehended by him, which was his life. But his life, as he looked at it, had no meaning as a separate life. It had meaning only as a part of a whole, of which he was at all times conscious. His words and actions flowed from him as smoothly, as inevitably, and as spontaneously, as the perfume rises from the flower" (p. 906).

This last passage is on a page marked by Galdós.[17] Curiously, he gave the nickname "Platon" to a character of *Fortunata and Jacinta*, explaining humorously that he was so called because he ate from a "large plate" (*platón;* as a proper noun "Plato"). The Spanish personage has none of the spiritual grace of Karataev, but it seems that the name "Platon" stuck in Don Benito's memory from his reading of Tolstoy.

Tolstoy reduced free will to "an infinitesimal minimum" (p. 1134) in human acts, but he did recognize it had some power to initiate men's behavior. He recognizes two kinds of activity — personal, that is, based on free choice, and "the life of the swarm," which is subject to historical laws (p. 565). There is a "fatalism in history" (p. 565), which Tolstoy sometimes equates with Providence,[18] just as Galdós did even before his acquaintance with *War and Peace* (see above, p. 46). Over centuries and millenia, God controls the direction of events (p. 1117, marked by Galdós) but the Deity does not intervene in everyday affairs (p. 1109, marked by Galdós).

In *Fortunata and Jacinta* these same ideas reappear. Maxi Rubín thinks about "the causes which order the universe and impose on the physical as well as the moral world a solemn, regular, and mathematical movement," and, in view of these laws, he exclaims, "Everything that should happen, happens and everything that should be, is."[19] Galdós comments, "He had conceived a blind faith in the direct action of Providence on the mechanism of everyday life. Providence dictated not only public but also private history" (*O.C.*, V, 225b). Maxi's thought agrees with Tolstoy, since both see Providence as the ultimate controlling force, working through inflexible laws. Maxi seems to reveal the author's intention, namely, to show that historical determinism (which Tolstoy found characteristic of the history of *nations*) is also applicable to the smallest unit, the *family*.[20]

Although Galdós speaks of "the direct action of Providence on the mechanism of everyday life," this does not mean a capricious intervention through miracles (which are a negation of laws). A little after the passage just cited, Fortunata, kneeling before the Host in the chapel, drifts into a dreamlike state in which she believes that God's voice speaks to her, chiding her for wanting to marry Juanito, a man far above her social rank. The Deity says, "I cannot alter my works or ride roughshod over my own laws" (249a). In short, God renounces his power to perform miracles; by this assumption Galdós can reconcile God's Providence with the determination of natural laws.

In novels written after *Fortunata and Jacinta* there is further evidence of Tolstoyan influence.[21] We should not, however, think that *War and Peace* is the only literary work which left traces in Don Benito's great work. Tolstoy's novel deserves all the attention we give it because it brought out the spiritual orientation which was gradually to increase in later Galdosian works. But we must not think of it so much as the cause of a new spiritual orientation as the catalytic agent which brought some of Galdós's own thought into sharper definition.

II   *The Story of Two Women*

Juanito Santa Cruz, an idle, pampered son of a well-to-do family of cloth merchants, is the man who links together the fortunes of the two women who give their names to the novel. Fortunata is the girl of the common people whom Juanito seduces with promises of marriage;[22] Jacinta is his cousin whom he marries.

On their wedding trip Jacinta little by little worms out of Juanito the story of his love affair with Fortunata, five months pregnant when he abandoned her (*O.C.*, V, 60). This is the beginning of the theme of maternity, which both divides and unites the two women. Jacinta is sterile and has a tremendous fixation on motherhood. In Madrid during trips into the slums on charity missions she meets Ido del Sagrario, whose diseased imagination creates a fiction that Fortunata's child by Juanito is living and is now in the care of Platón. To satisfy her great yearning for a child Jacinta buys the child from Platón[23] and tries to get Juanito and his parents to accept it. It is proved, however, that Juanito's real son has died.

Now Maxi Rubín enters the tale. He "was rachitic, of a poor and lymphatic constitution, absolutely devoid of personal attractions" (158b), a youth given to daydreaming, who "lived two existences, that of bread, and that of chimeras," and who in his imagination envisioned himself the object of a great love (163). After meeting Fortunata he idealizes her, seeks her regeneration by a stay in a convent (Las Micaelas), and finally marries her. Maxi is sick on their wedding night, and soon Fortunata, who has never stopped loving Juanito, falls again into his power. When Maxi tries to remonstrate, Juanito beats him up, and the marriage is broken off.

In the convent Fortunata has seen Jacinta among a group of society women who sponsor the work of the nuns. The sight of her rival produces a strange mixed emotion in the sinner. "That woman had robbed her of what in her opinion belonged rightfully to her. But another very different and more pronounced feeling was amalgamated strangely with this one. It was a most keen desire to resemble Jacinta, to be like her, to have her air, her charming appearance of sweetness and nobility. Because of all the ladies she saw that day none seemed to Fortunata so much a lady as Mrs. Santa Cruz" (243b). The unpolished girl of the slums begins to gravitate toward the refined lady of the upper class, whom she sees as a victim of Juanito just as she is (244a). Marriage, even to Maxi, she thinks will make her an "honest woman," hence more like Jacinta (244b).

After the impossible marriage of Fortunata and Maxi has been patched up and the couple is living together, there occurs another revealing episode between the two women. A common friend (Doña Guillermina, about whom we shall say more later) who is trying to counsel Fortunata yields reluctantly to Jacinta's desire and permits her to eavesdrop on the interview from a hiding place in the next room. To the consternation of Doña Guillermina, Fortunata declares that she is really Juanito's wife because of his promise to marry her and above all because she bore him a child (404b). Jacinta may be an angel, true, "but she has no children. A wife who has no children is not a wife" (405a). Soon after, Jacinta comes out of her hiding place and in an angry tirade abuses her rival in words which would be used by a woman of the common people. The civilized lady reveals an underlying natural stratum close to Fortunata's primitive emotional possessiveness.

During the interview Fortunata reveals that Juanito is pursuing her again and that she has an idea, not expressly stated, but that is something "which must be because it is so ordained" (406b). She goes back to her lover, exclaiming "it had to be. It's my destiny. . . . And I'm not sorry about it because I've got my idea here [in my mind], you know" (412b - 413a).

We learn exactly what her idea is when she becomes pregnant again. "You see how I achieved my idea" (470b). Her child will prove her claim that she is Juanito's real wife. The baby will, according to written law, have Rubín as his name, but by the law of nature he is a Santa Cruz (497b). Nevertheless, Fortunata is distraught with another great anxiety. Juanito has taken another mistress (Aurora), and there is the possibility he will have other children by her (524b). Fortunata rushes out to give Aurora a beating. Jacinta, for all her refinement, rejoices in Fortunata's act (528b). And Fortunata declares that one of the reasons why she roughed up Aurora was that the latter had cast suspicion on Jacinta's virtue (531b).

But the extreme exertion so soon after the delivery of her child brings Fortunata to the point of death. She sends the baby to Jacinta, telling her in a note that this child is not false, like the first one Jacinta wanted to adopt, but "legitimate and *natural*, as you will see in his face," where Juanito's traits are visible (537b). On receiving the child Jacinta was surprised "to perceive in her heart feelings which were something more than pity for the unfortunate woman, for there was perhaps, deep within her, something of comradeship, of fraternity, based on common misfortunes" (542b). Before long she thinks of herself as the flesh and blood mother of the baby (543b) and of Moreno Isla, her deceased platonic lover, as the father (544a) instead of Juanito, with whom she is no longer intimate.

III *Natural Love*

Behind the misadventures of the two women lies the conflict between natural and social law,[24] between free love and the institution of marriage. We must not take Fortunata's concept of free love as an endorsement for promiscuousness. Although she has had many men since the first episode with Juanito, she loves only Santa Cruz and regards him as her husband. "*You* are my husband . . . [and] all the others, nothing at all" (278a). Even after her marriage to Maxi, she feels that her real husband is her first lover and that she is fatally united to him forever (404b). So when Juanito calls her back she yields without hesitation, considering herself something "like a blind mechanism which is moved by a supernatural hand. What she had done she did, in her opinion, through the disposition of the mysterious forces which control the greatest things of the universe, the rising of the sun and the falling of heavy objects. She could not fail to do it, nor did she question the inevitable" (277a, see also 289b).[25]

Her love is all impulse, essentially romantic, akin to the mating of animals. Santa Cruz describes her as "a cute little animal, a savage who didn't know how to read or write. . . . But a good heart, a good heart" (50a). For her "love redeems all irregular conduct, better said, love makes everything regular for it rectifies laws, annulling those which oppose it" (323a).

She is, of course, a representative of the common people, a class which Galdós now envisions with some of the mystique we see in the Russian novelists, specifically in Tolstoy's treatment of Platon Karataev. Guillermina Pacheco upbraids her mentally, thinking: "You have no moral sense; you can never have principles because you are before civilization; you are a savage and belong completely to primitive stages of humanity"; but, because Fortunata would never understand these concepts, she only says, "You have the passions of the common people, crude and like a block of unworked stone." Galdós's comments on Guillermina's thought and speech: "This was true because the common people, in our [modern] societies, keep elemental ideas and sentiments in their rough plenitude, as the quarry contains marble, the matter [capable] of form. The common people possess great truths in block, and civilization has recourse to them as the little truths by which it lives are used up" (407a, see also 277b and 330a). In more specific terms, socialized love (marriage) cannot succeed without some of the primitive passion in which Fortunata believes. It is precisely because of this lack that her marriage to Maxi fails; he is capable of a profound and lasting love (343b and 546b), but he is impotent (181 and 473a). And should another elemental drive be frustrated (Jacinta's desire for children) that marriage is also incomplete.

Among the many secondary and minor characters that surround the central figure (Fortunata) we shall see a number who try to "civilize" her. There is, however, one who supports and reinforces her idea that nothing connected with love can be a sin (173b). This individual is Mauricia la dura (the "toughie"), an alcoholic whom Fortunata met in the convent for fallen women, and toward whom she felt an instinctive, inexplicable attraction. Mauricia exercised a strange and powerful fascination on her friend who could never figure out just why. "Things of the spirit, that only God understands!" (369b) she exclaims and tells Doña Guillermina "something extraordinary happened to me respecting that woman. Knowing that she was very bad, I loved her . . . I liked her and I couldn't help it. When she told me the terrible things she did in her life, I don't know. . . . I enjoyed listening to her . . . and when she advised me [to do] bad things, it seemed to me, in my inmost mind, it seemed to me that they weren't so bad and that she was right in recommending them to me. How do you explain this?" (398b).[26]

Mauricia can give her friend much information about the Santa Cruz family (she was reared in Doña Guillermina's house, next door to the Santa Cruz residence). Hence she can assure Fortunata that Juanito will return to her (246b) and that he has taken steps to seduce her the second time (264b). Above all, on her deathbed she proclaims that Fortunata will not sin in loving Juanito (370 and 379b). Mauricia, despite her Napoleonic countenance, her harsh voice, and her drunkenness, is Fortunata's authority in matters of love (246a).

IV *Civilizing Influences*

Doña Lupe, Maxi's widowed aunt, acts as a mother to her orphaned nephew, satisfying a strong maternal instinct (198b) as well as her dominant passion for directing other people's lives (199a). When she discovers that Fortunata wants to learn, "that she is a savage who needs to be domesticated" (244a), her gifts as an educator and counselor are aroused. She accedes to the marriage, which she knows has almost no chance of success, simply because she thinks she can train Fortunata just as she is molding Papitos (her servant girl) and her nephew.

There is a great deal of educating and training to be done. Fortunata, like other women of her class, does not know the meaning of many fairly common words or the order of the months of the year (173a and 178b). Even before Doña Lupe gets to know her Maxi has been teaching her how to write and the rudimentary facts generally known to a school boy. Doña Lupe sees that "She had to teach her everything: manners, language, conduct. The more poverty of education the pupil revealed, the more the teacher delighted in the perspectives and illusions of her plan" (261b - 262a).

But Fortunata runs off with Juanito soon after her wedding and for the time Doña Lupe's desires are frustrated. Shortly afterward, abandoned by her lover, she is taken in by Don Evaristo Feijoo, an elderly bachelor who leads a quiet, well-ordered existence, living on his pension as a retired colonel of the army (295a). He becomes a half-father, half-lover to Fortunata, while at the same time he is the author's philosopher of free love. He recognizes that "it is a great stupidity to rebel against Nature. It has its laws, and he who ignores them, pays for it" (337b). One of these natural laws is the nondura-tion of love, so that infidelity in marriage is nothing but nature demanding its rights against social despotism (339a). But one must compromise with the social rules, which means one must maintain appearances. This is the cardinal point in Don Evaristo's credo. Natural love, he agrees with Fortunata, is not a sin, but decorum must be maintained (334a). "You must give the heart its bits of flesh; it is a wild beast and long hunger infuriates it; but you must also give society's beast the part which corresponds to it so it won't start a dis-turbance" (341a). With these words the retired colonel, soon in-capable of sustaining the lover's role, is preparing Fortunata for a return to Maxi. In a sense he is half socializing her by advising her to keep her powerful natural love hidden, never ignoring "the holy appearances," the "external cult" of society "without which we would return to the state of savages" (353b).[27]

In fact, after her return to her husband and the further civilizing influences of Doña Lupe, Fortunata does not forget the doctrine of appearances. Juanito seduces her for the third time and while she yields immediately to her fated love, she remembers Feijoo's advice (413). Had she not become pregnant (her way of proving her natural claim to be Juanito's wife) her relations with her lover could have continued indefinitely.

A much more conventional socializing influence on Fortunata is exerted by Doña Guillermina Pacheco. This maiden lady has devoted her life to charity; her crowning achievement is the es-tablishment of an orphan asylum for which she begs and wheedles alms from both friends and strangers.[28]

In the structure of the novel she is a bridge between the lower classes, among whom she is constantly going on charitable missions, and the well-to-do. Her house adjoins the Santa Cruz residence and she is an intimate friend of the family. Jacinta accompanies her at times in her excursions into the slums or to the convent of Las Micaelas. Her nephew, the rich banker Moreno Isla, becomes a frustrated lover of Jacinta.

As Mauricia *la dura* lies dying, Guillermina cares for her, both attending to her physical wants and arranging for the proper religious rites. Fortunata also visits her dying friend; observing Guillermina's lively activity "she felt in her soul so much admiration

for that woman that she would have kissed the hem of her dress"
(368b). Guillermina becomes aware of Fortunata's identity after a
chance meeting at Mauricia's flat between the two rivals, during
which Fortunata abuses Jacinta. This leads to conferences between
the saint and the sinner, in which Guillermina upholds the priority of
social law over the impulses of the heart (397b and 407a). But
curiously, although Fortunata resents the advice Guillermina gives
her, she identifies her with her deceased friend Mauricia and
transfers to her "the mysterious sympathy" which the latter had inspired in her (400a). This begins when Fortunata lies in bed in a
twilight sleep and envisages the saint with Mauricia's features and
voice. Significantly, it is at this very moment that the idea of proving
her honorable place in society by bearing Juanito a son takes shape
in Fortunata's mind (399b). It is a subconscious melding of
Mauricia's declaration that love cannot be a sin and Guillermina's
exhortation to obey the canons of society. The net result of Doña
Guillermina's advice is not what she intended. By upholding the
rights of the legitimate wife she simply strengthens Fortunata's
resolve that she, too, has claims to an honorable status, based on the
laws of nature, through maternity.

V *Jacinta*

Compared to Fortunata, the woman of the common people, Jacinta is a rather pale figure, just as virtue and conventional conduct is
always less exciting than vice and rebelliousness. But, of all the
socializing influences on Fortunata, Jacinta, as a model, is the most
powerful. The "mania of imitation" is so strong that Fortunata
proposes to her husband that they adopt a child (392b), if possible
the very boy that Jacinta had tried to adopt (394a). Again, "emula-
tion or the imitative mania" makes her say that if her husband
became very sick she would devote herself unreservedly to caring for
him. "And then *that* woman would see if here [in me] there are
perfections or not" (391b), she thinks, as her hatred of her rival combines with her admiration.

Jacinta, like any human being, has natural physical and emotional
drives, especially her intense maternal instinct, which makes her try
to save a kitten lost in a sewer (71b) or dream that she is nursing a
baby (87b). She feels extreme jealousy when she overhears Fortunata's claim to be the real wife of Juanito. While she is capable of
imagining that Moreno Isla, not Juanito, is the father of the baby
Fortunata gives her (see p. 95), she has always refrained from giving

her admirer any positive indication of the esteem, bordering on love, which she felt for him (449b - 461). In other words, Jacinta's feelings are usually cloaked under social propriety. Living as she does in the household of Juanito's parents, she cannot talk to them about the infidelities of their son.

Aurora, at the time still Fortunata's friend, accuses Jacinta of having an affair with Moreno Isla (444a), himself a great believer in social propriety. The effect of this slander of Jacinta on Fortunata is devastating. If the angel, the model of virtue has fallen, what difference is there between the paramour and the legal wife? Social law no longer exists, only love, the natural law, reigns (444b).

Fortunata makes the mistake of telling Juanito that his wife is unfaithful and gets an angry denial for her pains (463). Soon afterward Aurora changes her story: Jacinta is virtuous although she may have looked at the banker with a certain sympathy (465b). "What difference does it make to you if she is honorable or not? What matters to you is that he loves you more than her" says Aurora. " 'Oh, no!' exclaimed Fortunata with her whole soul. 'If that woman were not honorable it would seem to me that there is no honor in the world' " (466a). So the woman who has declared that love is the supreme law now maintains that social law is of at least equal importance. Fortunata has come a long way toward society's standards.

VI *Maxi*

Maxi's tragedy is that he is "all spirit" (167a) but only "half a man" physically (224b; also 183b, 281b, and 473a). Doctor Augusto Miquis, had he been consulted, would have advised him peremptorily to remain unmarried (283b). A dreamer, he sees "things through the lense of his own ideas," which made all appear as it ought to be and not as it is (189a). He is of course another example of a person deluded by giving way to his imagination, and so he conceives that he has a "mission" — like the romanticists — to redeem the fallen woman (189b).

If Galdós has often condemned imagination (see p. 36), he now sees its workings in a new and different light. The idea of a successful marriage with Fortunata was a mad, impossible dream, and Maxi was a fool to entertain it. "But he was not an ordinary fool; he was one of those fools who touch the sublime with their finger tips. It's true that they don't grasp it, but they *do* touch it" (190a). Imagination leads him out of reality into a dream world, but imagination also lets him see Fortunata as a human being, his equal, not an outcast from society. It is the faculty through which the spirit must operate, for all activity which originates within a person (not determined by outside causes) must be imagined as a first step toward its consummation. Galdós has given ground on his distrust of imagination; in later works he will give more and more value to the combination of imagination and spirit.

So Maxi is a kind of poet as he perceives a possible "honorability of the soul" in Fortunata (165a) and when he declares to his aunt that he feels "a very great force" within him which impels him to her salvation (201a). Viewed from a different angle, Maxi's dream is to socialize his adored one. He counts on the force of his love, just as powerful and unswerving as Fortunata's for Juanito, as the agent which will ultimately make her his and give her an honorable place in society. For his love is the very core of his being. Wise Don Evaristo, urging Fortunata to return to her husband, tells her, "Don't you see he is like you a passionate, sentimental man? He idolizes you and those who love in that way, madly, are eager to forgive" (343b). Maxi himself tells her that "the world is worth nothing except through love" (391b) and Fortunata also realizes, even as she leaves him for the third time, that this "poor little fellow" is "the only one who has truly loved me, the one who has pardoned me two times and would pardon me the third . . . and the fourth" (469a).

Maxi goes literally mad from love and contemplates liberation through suicide (432). Fortunata's death removes the cause of his aberration so that after viewing her tomb he can calmly survey their relationship. He tells his friend: "I loved her with my whole soul. I made of her the capital object of my life, and she did not respond to my desires. . . . I made a mistake, and she did too. I wasn't the only one deceived; she was also. We defrauded each other reciprocally. We did not count on Nature, which is the great mother and teacher that rectifies the errors of her wayward children. We do a thousand foolish things and she corrects them for us" (546b).

These words are the author's summing up of the conflict between natural and social laws, represented by free love and marriage. Galdós was a realist in his philosophic outlook as well as in literature. He knew that many idealistic goals could not be reached in the Spain of his time, no matter how worthy they might be. We already saw him telling political liberals, whose ideals he shared, to await a propitious time for acting (see p. 43). Later, he wrote two novels in which he says that the Tolstoyan injunction "Resist not evil" simply will not work.[29] A third novel, *Tristana*, deals with woman's emancipation but concludes that feminism, a movement with which Don Benito sympathized, is bound to be defeated in late nineteenth-century Spain. Galdós will not let idealism sweep him away. He keeps his feet firmly planted on the ground.

Maxi's dream is condemned to frustration by the *données* in which the author states his problem. Not only is Maxi impotent (or at least very nearly so) but Fortunata cannot stop loving Juanito, no matter how badly he treats her. Consequently nature must necessarily overcome society, as Maxi finally realizes.

A couple of pages after his calm and sane evaluation of his marriage, at the very end of the novel, Maxi expresses the wish to retire to a monastery. They take him to Leganés, the insane asylum near Madrid. He exclaims: "These fools probably think they are deceiving me! This is Leganés. I accept it, I accept it and say nothing, as a proof of the absolute submission of my will to whatever the world wishes to do with my person. They will not shut my thought within walls. I reside in the stars. Let them put the man called Maximiliano Rubín in a palace or in a dung heap. . . . It's all the same" (547b).

This passage, which shows Maxi achieving a spiritual peace, indifferent to the material world, can be compared to a famous scene in *War and Peace*,[30] in which Pierre realizes that there is a "force of life" which works against the deterministic law of history. A prisoner of the French, forced to march away from Moscow, poorly fed, and bivouacing in the cold, Pierre realizes "that just as there is no position in the world in which a man can be happy and perfectly free, so too there is no position in which he need be unhappy and in bondage" (988; Galdós turned down the following page). Sitting on the cold ground, leaning against a wagon wheel, he bursts into laughter, and says, "They have taken me — shut me up. They keep me prisoner. Who is 'me'? Me — my immortal soul! Ha, ha, ha!" For the present writer there is an undeniable similarity between Maxi and Pierre's reaction to imprisonment. Both come to the identical conclusion that spiritual peace is all that matters and that material conditions are of no importance.

Although of course there are numerous ways in which the two men differ, the spiritual naturalism of both authors is incarnated principally in these two figures.

VI   *Secondary Characters and Settings*

Our discussion of *Fortunata and Jacinta* up to this point could give the impression of an "abstract" novel, where all the characters represent social or moral forces. In fact, the author's thought is so thoroughly concealed that the casual reader is almost unaware of the serious content. This is due to the great interest of the secondary characters and in the scene of action in Madrid.

Some of these secondary characters are needed for the mechanics of the plot. For example, Plácido Estupiñá, formerly an employee of Jacinta's father, is another link between the inhabitants of the low quarters and the Santa Cruz family. He can give Doña Barbarita (Juanito's mother) information about the places and persons her son frequents when she suspects, from his use of low-class turns of speech,[31] that he is having an affair with a girl of the common people. His role is particularly important when Fortunata, about to have her baby, returns to her old home high over the Plaza Mayor and finds that Estupiñá lives on the floor beneath her. Thus communication is established through him with Doña Guillermina and Jacinta.

But the author does not limit himself to Estupiñá's function as a tie between persons of different classes. He devotes many pages, including one long chapter (34 - 42), to this loquacious personage, who failed in various businesses simply because he could not stop talking long enough to make a sale. All this does not further the plot, but it is a delight to the reader.[32] Galdós dwells lovingly on Estupiñá, giving him more space than his importance in the novel's structure deserves.

The same can be said of Maxi's aunt and his two brothers. One of the latter, Juan Pablo, is prominent as a café philosopher. Galdós uses this character skillfully as an ironic restatement on a lower plane, of the principal themes of his work. First we see Juan Pablo as the leader of a group of café habitués who move suddenly and mysteriously from one favorite coffee house to another. "The changes were determined by certain migratory currents which exist in the society of idlers and of which no one can explain the origin" (293b). Such a trivial thing as café life has its "historical laws" and like those of history in the large sense, they are still only half revealed.

In discussions with his friends Juan Pablo defends free love (494b) but hardly has he received a position as a provincial governor (499) than he becomes a stout defender of social values (500a) and abjures his relationship with his mistress, our old acquaintance Refugio Sánchez Emperador (501b). He has been "socialized," although his motives are of the basest sort.

The other brother, Nicolás, is a priest, who furthers the narrative by arranging for Fortunata's admission to Las Micaelas. He becomes a canon (despite his gross, bestial customs) because Fortunata gets Feijoo to use his influence to obtain the appointment. When the news reaches her Fortunata muses: "There are two societies, the one that is visible and the one that is hidden. If it hadn't been for my sinful conduct when would this stupid, ordinary, foul-smelling man have become a canon? And he so satisfied" (388b). The events of history sometimes have obscure causes, and the acts of the most humble person sometimes determine results of consequence (see p. 46). We could go on talking about secondary and minor characters indefinitely as they are numerous, well drawn, and an attractive part of the leisurely paced novel. We could also mention the large number of repeated characters from earlier works, generally just named in passing. But we must turn to the setting and background of *Fortunata and Jacinta.*

The fathers of both Juanito and Jacinta are cloth merchants. They live in the area between the Plaza Mayor and the Puerta del Sol, where even today the same merchandise is sold. Galdós goes into the history of the two families, which is simultaneously a history of the cloth trade with the changes of popularity of certain materials and the increasing demand for imported novelties (chap. 2).[33] In fact the cloth trade runs through the whole novel. Estupiñá calls Doña Barbarita's attention to some new cretonnes (74a); Jacinta is dazzled by the brightly colored materials hanging on display before the shops of the low quarters (99a); Aurora opens an establishment for the sale of white goods (389a) in which she introduces many Parisian novelties (424). Even political changes are fomented by cloth merchants and tailors, since each change of regime means another group of bureaucrats can afford new clothes (344b).

The area in which the cloth trade is located is only a few minutes walk from the low quarters, the habitat of the common people, where Fortunata, Platón, and Estupiñá live. It is easy for Juanito to go to the taverns and houses of questionable morality. But Galdós assures us that there are many links between the have-nots and the successful businessmen. Almost every family has branches in both areas and in both social categories (66a - 68a), which the author views as a good thing (65b), consonant with his belief that ultimately

Spanish society will be fused in a single class (see p. 44). All this background material is a sort of sociological analysis of the relations between the classes of the population of Madrid. The descriptions of individuals of the different classes and the environments they frequent is in the best manner of *costumbrismo*, dwelling on local color and humorously presented picturesque traits. One learns a great deal about Madrid from the details that Galdós assembled in this work.[34]

VII *Technique*

In the same way that Ido del Sagrario and Felipe Centeno argued about the aesthetic worth of realism and idealism (see p. 74), a pair of characters debate the possibility of using Fortunata's story as literary material (544a). One of them, a literary critic, maintains that it would be necessary to add imaginary episodes to dress up commonplace real happenings. "He wouldn't tolerate life being turned into art just as it is, but [wanted it] arranged, seasoned with sweet-smelling spices and thoroughly cooked." His interlocutor prefers the raw fruit.

Galdós is judging his own work in this little dialogue and clearly prefers the unadorned subject matter of everyday life, presented in the language of living people in ordinary conversations. He does use, however, a couple of modern stylistic devices. He has Moreno Isla indulge in a long mental soliloquy (445), which amounts to a stream of consciousness, a device whose first manifestation is usually thought to be later than this novel. He employs the "double stream of narrative" effectively, when, for example, he interlards Jacinta's honeymoon trip with Juanito's confession of his seduction of Fortunata. He fixes the time of the fictitious events by references to current history, often with an ironical parallelism.[35] Humor pervades many scenes. When Mauricia announces solemnly that she has seen the Virgin (252b) the whole convent (Las Micaelas) hesitates between mystic exaltation and incredulity. Could such a sinner be so favored? Then the truth comes out: she has filched a bottle of cognac (257). All her mysticism was alcoholic. After a great brawl Mauricia is thrown out into the street.

Humor also underlies the chapter heading "Naturalismo espiritual," a phrase so closely associated with the author's viewpoint in this work. (Incidentally, we have here a good example of his ability to laugh at things he takes seriously.) In the chapter so entitled, Mauricia is dying. She receives the sacraments of the church (the "spiritual" element), but she also advises Fortunata to continue her affair with Juanito (the naturalistic element). At the last moment, when Guillermina eases her death with a draught of sherry, she utters her last word, a word which some think is "More" and others hear as "Now." Is it "more wine" or "now I see heaven and the angels"?

Among the many writings devoted entirely or partially to *Fortunata and Jacinta* [36] there is one which deals primarily with the structure of the novel.[37] Gullón finds two superimposed structural elements: the good (Guillermina) — bad (Mauricia), and a shifting triangular interest in three principal characters at one time, of whom Fortunata is always one. Many of his observations concur with points of view set forth above. Another theory of the structure of the novel was advanced at the meeting of the Modern Language Association in December, 1972. Vernon A. Chamberlin's paper was predicated on Galdós's great admiration for Beethoven and specifically on the structural similarities between the *Eroica* symphony and *Fortunata*. We hope his theory will be published in complete detail in the near future.

The new spiritual element which infused the naturalism of Galdós's great novel has already been clearly seen by others, notably by the well-known critic Joaquín Casalduero: "Galdós felt the need of going beyond the naturalistic concept of the world when he created *Fortunata and Jacinta*, because the clash between Fortunata and Jacinta sets forth a conflict which naturalism cannot by itself reveal. The opposed worlds of these two women go beyond the material wall which surrounds them, and on spreading beyond, show themselves subjected to a spiritual force which Galdós could not fail to see . . . since naturalism was to rediscover the Spirit. . . . In *Fortunata and Jacinta*, then, Galdós's naturalistic phase ends and his new cycle begins, which is characterized by the presence of the Spirit."[38]

VIII   Miau *(Meow)*

In *Fortunata and Jacinta* Galdós introduced a minor figure named Ramón Villamil, nicknamed Ramsés II because of his dried-up, mummylike appearance.[39] He now brings him into a new novel as a protagonist. Villamil's problem is that he has lost his job in the tax collection agency of the Treasury Ministry. He is a *cesante*, a former bureaucrat who must wait until a change of government restores him to his position. Don Ramón's tragedy is that he needs only two months of active service to be pensioned off with four-fifths of his salary. Despite his long years of scrupulously honest devotion to his office, he remains unemployed until he finally seeks liberation from his misery through suicide.

Part of his problem is his family, especially his wife (Pura), who is as pretentious as Rosalía de Bringas. She is willing to pawn everything in their flat with the exception of the furniture and draperies of the sitting room, which she retains in order to impress visitors.[40] The family group also includes Abelarda (Pura and Ramón's daughter), whom Galdós repeatedly calls "the insignificant girl" because of her lack of both physical and intellectual graces; and Luis, the nine-year-old grandson of Don Ramón, who has almost equal prominence with his grandfather in the narrative.

Luis is indignant because his schoolmates tease him with the nickname "Miau" which has been fastened on the family because of the feline appearance of the three women. He even gets into a fist fight with one of his friends because of these taunts (378). Later, when Villamil presents his scheme of reform of the tax structure to a group of treasury employees, one joker points out that the initial letters of his four recommendations (Morality, Income tax, Aduanas [Customs], and Unification of national debts) spell out the word "MIAU" (494 - 95). The heartless bureaucrats ridicule the old public servant, whom the author constantly compares to an old, decrepit tiger, thus endowing him with the catlike appearance of the family (321). Perhaps the author wished to make the Villamil family representative of all the inhabitants of Madrid whose nickname, probably because of their nocturnal habits, is "cats" (*gatos madrileños*).

Don Ramón is convinced that it is useless to hope for reemployment, although he continually writes letters to persons of influence to try to be reinstated. He sees examples of men junior to him in years of service going to positions higher than the one he had filled, and he even sees some men known to have defrauded the Treasury raised to places of importance through the pressures exerted by influential people, particularly women. The final disillusionment comes when Victor Cadalso (the husband of Villamil's deceased daughter Luisa and the father of Luis) arrives in Madrid pursued by charges of having embezzled tax collections. The accusation is patently true, yet Victor pulls strings to escape punishment and is appointed to a better job in the Treasury Department.

Villamil and his family had many reasons to hate Victor. With his Andalusian loquacity he had fascinated Luisa, and by treating her with shabby indifference had strained her unbalanced, imaginative nature to the point of insanity and death (418 - 21). Victor is a study in contrasts: his handsome, noble external appearance covers a vicious, Mephistophelian personality. Above all he is a consummate actor (390 and 510), using his command of language (396) to cajole and delude. During the action time of the novel he uses his diabolical power of expression to beguile Abelarda (394, 439, and 473), deceiving her with declarations of love based on his readings of romantic novels (442 and 472). When she leaves home to elope with him, he brushes her off, leaving her so upset mentally that she attacks and almost kills Luis, evidently a surrogate figure for his father (582, 625 and 639). Her attempt to choke the little boy ends in an epileptic seizure (626), an episode similar to what had happened to Luisa not long before her death (421). We shall see Luis and Don Ramón also suffering from mental aberrations, clearly an example of a family flaw so dear to the naturalists.

Luis is prone to a kind of fainting (the *petit mal* of epilepsy), which at the time of our story involves his extreme concern over his grandfather's lack of employment. During his seizures he has a vision of a white-bearded old man, somewhat like an old beggar he has seen (332). The apparition, whom he thinks is God, relates Ramón's problem to Luis's failure to study his lessons for school, implying that Luis can bring about his grandfather's reappointment by concentrating on his books. After his first vision, as subsequently, he has doubts (337 and 384); yet ultimately he is convinced that he has really talked with God.

Galdós presents the appearances of the godlike figure with delightful humor. Since Villamil is constantly writing letters to government officials, Luis seems to see "God" writing letters to the Treasury Minister (350). When the teacher catches Luis distracting the class with cigar bands on his fingers, "God" next appears with the same type of rings, but now made of precious metals and gems (381 - 82). Obviously events and worries of the boy's real life enter his visions. Finally "God" seems to be an ideal "old grandfather" (638) rather than the beggar that first gave rise to the vision. Luis now confidently tells him that all family problems would be solved if only Ramón were given work. "God" replies that the Minister of the Treasury did not obey his order and that Villamil will never be reappointed. The best thing the grandfather can do is to die, and Luis is to tell him so (639 - 40).

Since all of Luis's visions are based on elements of the real world it seems to us that the grandson has sensed the old man's desperation and his resolve to seek liberation in suicide. The author has shown us Villamil frequenting the government offices, where he finds less and less comprehension of his tax reform plans. Idle employees, spending their time drinking coffee and joking, ridicule him increasingly. Higher officials begin to show irritation at his importunate visits. Even his good friend Pantoja cannot understand his proposals for change, especially the income tax (596).

Pantoja is the model of administrative honorability and application to duty (482 - 84) and at the same time supremely narrow-minded in his concept of his functions (486 - 87). He is introduced into the narrative as a foil to Villamil, his equal in scrupulous devotion to duty but his opposite as the advocate of new tax laws. As Don Ramón shows increasing signs of an unbalanced mind, he is another example of Quixotic "method in madness" *(la razón de la sinrazón)* that we have seen in Jesús Delgado and in Maxi Rubín. Like the former, he is ahead of his times (the income tax was not introduced into Spain until 1900 and then in a limited form). Similarly to Maxi Rubín, who for a while believed in liberation from the world's wickedness through suicide, Villamil not only believes in but practices this conviction.

Don Ramón is losing his mental equilibrium (536 and 674). Finally having made up his mind to take his life he exclaims: "Thank God I have had the courage to cast off my chain and recover my personality" (662). Although he suffers momentary doubts, he refers several times to the liberty and peace his resolution will bring him (651, 657, 660, and 664). At this point Luis's report that "God" thinks that he, Villamil, should die reinforces his determination.

Enjoying a new-found freedom Don Ramón wanders on the outskirts of Madrid during his last afternoon of life. He observes the beauties of nature, which his worries had kept from him. He feels supremely happy (656) and in a tavern enjoys a meal which tastes far better than the food he has been eating (657). His spirit is free (660). Commending himself to God and to his grandson, whom he sees as a saint (676), he shoots himself.

Villamil's self-liberation, although the product of a disturbed mind, must be seen as part of Galdós's trend toward greater spirituality. Here is a man who refuses to have both body and spirit imprisoned, although to free the spirit he must destroy the body. Certain similarities to Pierre's declaration of spiritual freedom are evident — an awareness of the beauties of nature and the relishing of simple pleasures. As Joaquín Casalduero writes: "This spiritual element [of *Fortunata and Jacinta*] becomes more perceptible in *Miau* and is completely evident in *Realidad*."[41]

Ricardo Gullón has pointed out similarities between *Meow* and Balzac's *Les employés*.[42] The Balzacian hero, Rabourdin, like Villamil, is a bureaucrat who proposes administrative reforms, is ridiculed, and fails, while an unscrupulous rival triumphs. But Balzac's employee attains wealth and happiness outside of the world of government offices, whereas the Spaniard can find only a few hours of happiness at the price of renouncing his world — the office and the family, now seen as absurd and evil — and by removing himself violently from their control. *Meow* probably owes some suggestions to *Les Employés*, but it is by no means an imitation.

The unemployed bureaucrat was a frequent subject of *costumbrista* essays and even appeared in an occasional novel.[43] Of course Galdós needed no source material as he was in the Congress (in the building of which one scene of *Meow* takes place), and he knew many politicians and bureaucrats. If for no other reason than to urge the appointment or advancement of friends, he had many occasions to visit government offices. He describes them vividly in this novel.

Meow falls short of the high level of excellence of *Fortunata and Jacinta*. It perhaps suffers precisely because it comes after a masterpiece. But judged in isolation, it must be called a very good novel.

CHAPTER 8

Spiritual Naturalism Continued

I La incógnita *and* Realidad

IN these two novels Galdós employs a clever new idea; that is, he tells the same story twice from different points of view. *La incógnita* (The Unknown) is presented as a mystery story in which an amateur detective (Manolo Infante) tries to find out if Federico Viera has been murdered or committed suicide. As implied in the title, the novel ends without solution, even though Infante collects all the external evidence possible. What is lacking is the internal evidence — the forces which motivated Federico and the people closely associated with him.

Hence the story can be retold stressing the spiritual drives that must be known to solve the mystery. The second version is aptly named *Realidad* (Reality). It marks the novelist's renunciation of one of the prime tenets of naturalism, the belief that all human activity results from the physical stimuli of heredity and environment, in a word, determinism. Infante had investigated the possible materialistic causes of Viera's death without reaching a conclusion. It is only when the characters reveal their aspirations, emotions, and dreams that the truth comes out.

In order to have them express their innermost selves Galdós chooses the dramatic form, writing his novel in five acts, using only dialogue, soliloquies, and stage directions. Perhaps we should say at once that the dramatic form brings with it difficulties. Galdós abuses the soliloquy in order to penetrate the subsurface motives of his personages.[1] He also employs numerous asides, so that a character in the physical presence of others speaks without being heard by them. Since the novel is meant to be read, not acted, we can think of these asides as the individual's silent thoughts. They become a real problem later, however, when Galdós converts *Reality* into a stage production. The same difficulty obtains for the apparitions or dream figures of the novel, a device which enables the author to have a solitary personage talk in a most revealing way with hallucinatory projections of other characters.

These observations apply, of course, only to *Reality*. *The Unknown* encounters no such difficulties because it is told strictly from a single point of view, and this restriction is imposed by couching it in a series of letters, written by Manolo Infante to a friend called X (suggesting the mathematical unknown). Infante can tell only what he sees and hears, and he never gets far enough below surface appearances to discover the truth.

Federico is a youngish bachelor who considers himself to be of the highest rank of the upper bourgeoisie. But he has practically no money and gambles continuously to try to alleviate his poverty, suffering alternate ups and downs of fortune. He sometimes borrows from La Peri,[2] a high-level courtesan, for whom he feels a deep fraternal attachment. He also frequents the social group (which includes Infante) that gathers in Tomás Orozco's house.

Now Orozco is a sort of Krausistic saint[3] — a layman who does much charitable work but who insists on remaining unknown as the benefactor and rejects all expressions of gratitude. His virtue and his aloofness from the objects of his charity make him a cold man, easier to admire than to love. His wife, Augusta, finds herself drifting away from him.

A swarm of admirers and would-be seducers (of whom Infante is one) surrounds Augusta. Infante thinks she favors Federico, and, after the latter's death, he is convinced that she knows how it happened. She, however, refuses to tell him anything substantive, limiting herself to the confession that she has not been chaste. Speculation on the reasons for, and manner of, Viera's demise is abundant. Numerous theories are advanced: Orozco (who in fact was away from Madrid on a hunting expedition) either murdered him or hired an assassin; a second unspecified lover of Augusta, jealous of Federico, killed him; Augusta murdered him out of jealousy of La Peri; and there were several other fantastic rumors. The one to which Manolo attributes "distant glimmers of truth" is as follows: Orozco surprises the lovers in their hideaway, draws a revolver and hands it to Federico saying: "the one who should die is you. If in your soul there is a spark of the sentiment of honor, you know what you have to do." Viera takes the weapon and kills himself.[4] In fact, this version is close to the truth; its only mistake is in having Orozco intervene directly.

At the end of *The Unknown* the narrator comments on the difference between his account and that of *Reality*, which his friend X has just sent him. It is the distinction between "the inner face" and "the outer face," "the profound truth" and "the apparent truth." Infante's narrative is only the empty shell, not the living creature dwelling within (207).

In *Reality* we learn that Orozco wants to give a small fortune to Federico, because the fathers of the two men had been business associates and an unpaid account has been discovered. The idea of accepting money from the man with whose wife he is having an affair drives Viera into such a nervous disequilibrium and fills him with such sentiments of shame and dishonor that he commits suicide. With the aid of a faithful servant Augusta is able to hide her participation as a witness of the suicide. Orozco guesses the truth and gives his wife a chance to confess to him and, as he says, "to raise herself to me by an act of noble contrition."[5] She denies categorically her presence at the scene of her lover's death (252): Orozco knows she is deceiving him and feels that a spiritual divorce exists between them, so he turns the conversation to inconsequential, everyday affairs, determined to reduce their marriage to a mere simulation (255 - 56).

But as he lies asleep that night the dream-image of Federico appears, and Orozco tells him that the cause of his death was shame and that he (Orozco) honors him for it. He praises Federico and declares "the star of good shines in your soul. You are one of my kind. Your death is a sign of moral greatness. I admire you and I want you to be my friend" (260).

The two men's spiritual stimuli are exactly opposite to the conventional Spanish reaction to a situation of wifely infidelity. Honor, as exemplified in the plays of Calderón, requires a husband to kill his wife or at least to entomb her in a convent; the "normal" seducer brags of his triumph and considers himself a most attractive fellow. Orozco simply divorces Augusta from his intimacy, and Federico, far from preening himself, is driven to self-destruction by shame.

The situation we have just described has marked similarities to one in Tolstoy's *Anna Karenina*. As the heroine lies apparently dying she demands that her husband give his hand to her lover (Vronsky). She calls Karenin a saint, and he forgives them both. Vronsky, moved by the magnanimity and grandeur of the husband, shoots himself with the full intention of ending his life, although his attempt is unsuccessful.[6] Karenin finds spiritual joy in his forgiveness, despite the disapproval of society and Anna's increasing fear of him which prompts her to say that she hates him for his virtue. No doubt Galdós could have found a suggestion of his plot in Tolstoy, although the question remains in dispute.[7]

The complexity of Galdós's "sources" is nowhere better illustrated than in *Reality*. One factor was a current event, a murder which absorbed everyone's attention from July 1, 1888 to May, 1889. Known as "the crime of Fuencarral Street," it provoked limitless speculation, investigative reporting, and even a special two-page supplement in *El Imparcial* (March 25, 1889 and following).

The murder itself was nothing unusual — an old woman was killed, and her servant (Higinia) confessed to having murdered her. But interest heightened when the accused changed her story and threw the blame on José Varela, the murdered widow's son. Then it became known that Varela was in jail, although many witnesses declared that they had seen him on the streets on the day of the crime. Since the victim's money and jewelry could not be found, it was hypothesized that another man — a Mister X — had to be involved.

Don Benito followed these events closely and sent articles about them to *La Prensa* of Buenos Aires.[8] He attended the trial, and in his report he speaks of "the slow revelation of the truth amid so many contradictory statements," the reconstruction of "the reality of the crime," and "the clarification of the unknown" (124 and 127 - 28). In the courtroom he studied Higinia's expression and tried to pierce her exterior calm to fathom her true nature (140). Surely the theme of the inner truth concealed under the surface appearances occurred to him as he watched the unfolding of the crime of Fuencarral Street. But Galdós did not get the specific kind of crime from the real-life event. No suggestion of Orozco's rejection of the conventional *pundonor* or Viera's remorseful suicide exists in the crime of Fuencarral Street.

As if this were not enough, other sources have been advanced. Bourget's psychological novel is one,[9] Ibsen's undramatic drama, with its emphasis on deep-lying psychological motives, is another. The latter became prominent when *Reality* was produced on the stage (1892) and Galdós was hailed as "the Spanish Ibsen."[10] By the time of the staging of *Reality* the Norwegian playwright was well-known in Spain, but such was not true when Don Benito composed *The Unknown* and *Reality*.[11] There is only an outside chance that he could have read a French translation of Ibsen at that time.[12]

Another matter is the extent to which Galdós drew on his own personality and parliamentary experiences in creating Manolo Infante. As in every case of autobiographical similarities we must not forget that there is no one-to-one correspondence between the living author and his creation. Yet both are representatives in the Congress, where Infante suffers terror on giving his unique speech.[13] Like Don Benito, he has so weak a voice that he cannot be heard throughout the room. And when Manolo first goes into society he feels "graceless and embarrassed."[14] Some social attitudes of Infante also correspond to Galdós's feelings: he sympathizes with the hard lot of the Castilian peasants and condemns absentee landlords; he approves of the marriage of Federico's sister to an ambitious but low-born young man, thus bringing about the fusion of classes which Galdós advocated persistently.[15]

Finally, there is an increased interest in the psychology of the subconscious. Infante has a revelation while in a twilight sleep which seems to him to be the indisputable truth; when he recounts it to his friend X, who can "penetrate the arcane of the human soul," he is surprised to find that X agrees with him and extols the power of intuition.[16] This element of the subconscious will increase in later Galdosian novels hand-in-hand with growing spirituality. Galdós has not ceased being a realist — in fact, in *The Unknown* (p. 165) he contrasts reality with imagination, pointing out that the tremendous variety of real creatures and human types surpasses the wildest dreams of the imagination. The only difference is that he now enlarges his concept of realism to include deep-lying psychological and spiritual forces. The gradual changes in his attitude toward reality are precisely the key to his thought development and the paramount interest in his changing life view.

II *Biographical Interlude*

We know more details about Galdós's life in the period 1885-1891 than in any period of similar length. As we have seen, he was in the Congress from 1886 to 1890. Some of the honorary duties of his position interested him more than the day by day routine of debates. He was among those delegated to receive the infant Alfonso XIII for the nation; he was part of a commission that visited the Exposition of Barcelona in May, 1888, where he was invited to dine with the Queen Regent and King Oscar of Sweden. The king's affability surprised and charmed Don Benito. While in Barcelona he also met and dined with the Catalan authors Narcis Oller and José Ixart, with the first of whom he had corresponded before.[17]

Galdós also traveled widely during the summers of the 1880s. In

1885 he went to Portugal with Pereda;[18] in 1886 he made an excursion to the Rhineland; in 1887 he went to England to meet his good friend José Alcalá Galiano and traveled with him through Holland, Germany, and Denmark;[19] in the autumn of 1888 he accompanied Alcalá Galiano on an excursion through Italy, where he visited many artistic sites.[20]

His travels in 1889 are worthy of especial note. As often, he went by ship to England to seek out Alcalá Galiano with the intention of going with him to the Paris Exposition. But his friend could not leave his consular post in Newcastle on Tyne, and Don Benito, after a few days in Edinburgh and a visit to Stratford to pay his respects to Shakespeare,[21] had to go to Paris alone. But he did not stay long in Paris; he went on to the Rhine valley, where he met Emilia Pardo Bazán and had a brief affair with her.[22]

Pardo Bazán had urged Galdós to write something for a new magazine (La España Moderna),[23] and he complied by publishing the short novel Torquemada en la hoguera (Torquemada in the Fire). A few years later he was to continue the story of this miserly character's life in three more volumes to which this first one serves as an introduction. Hence we shall reserve consideration of the series until we can see it as a whole.

The year 1889 also marks Galdós's election to the Royal Spanish Academy, a self-perpetuating group of thirty-six literary men. His first candidacy was voted down (Jan. 17) and in his stead the academy chose an unknown named Commelerán, whose only achievement was a Latin dictionary. Clearly the vote reflected the reactionary prejudice of many members against the novelist's liberal views. But as if ashamed of their bias they gave Don Benito an overwhelming approval when another vacancy occurred (June 13, 1889) and welcomed him to their corporation. Galdós, however, did not take his seat until 1897, owing in part to his timidity about making a public speech and perhaps partly to his resentment at having been passed over on the first vote.

Although Emilia Pardo Bazán strove to continue her amorous relation with Galdós he broke off their intimacy, remaining only a good friend. One chief reason for the rupture was his involvement with another woman, Lorenza Cobián, who became the mother of Galdós's daughter María. María was born Jan. 12, 1891, in Santander, and it is significant that Galdós remained in that city during the winter of 1890 - 91, contrary to his custom of spending only the summers there. His letters to Lorenza and María show a deep concern for their welfare and a sense of responsibility toward them. Lorenza died insane, committing suicide on July 25, 1906. Galdós continued to interest himself in María's education and made her the beneficiary of his will.[24]

III   Angel Guerra

Angel Guerra is a three-volume novel which revolves around an idealist in conflict with bourgeois mentality and all the injustice to which middle-class society closes its eyes. As a boy he witnessed the execution of a number of sergeants, shot because of their participation in a frustrated army coup. The experience had a profound and shattering effect on Angel; throughout his life a nightmare vision reappears to him at times of stress. He sees again a man whom he had observed at the execution, his eyes starting from their sockets, his hair literally standing on end, his face a Greek mask of horror. "This is infamous!" the dream figure shouts. The execution and its subconscious memory are the origin of Angel's revolutionary political idealism: "As the indelible traces of smallpox continue to exist in those who have suffered this cruel disease, so the imprint of that tremendous upheaval continued to exist in the psychological make-up of Angel Guerra" (1239b).

As the boy grows into a man he develops ambivalent feelings toward his mother, Doña Sales. She is a domineering, stern woman, who controls Angel even to the point of making him marry the girl of her choice. Doña Sales is surrounded by friends who share her respect for social conventions. As tensions become ever stronger, Angel describes her as the "personification of the social order" (1270b). A break is inevitable, although Angel has a great need for maternal love. Addressing her mentally he says, "I loved you and I respected you above all things and your will was sacred for me" (1250b).

When the novel opens, Angel, now a widower, has left home and has been living for a year with Dulce, a girl with a past but sincerely and lovingly devoted to him. He has just participated in an abortive revolutionary attempt to overthrow the government and was one of a group responsible for the death of an unarmed colonel, an event which fills him with guilt (1271b). He must soon return home at least long enough to get money from Doña Sales, for, although he is thirty years old and has a legal right to his inheritance, he has left it in his mother's hands. But the idea of confronting her terrifies him; he knows that she will upbraid him for his role in the revolutionary coup and for his devotion to Dulce. When he steels himself to return home he finds Doña Sales in imminent danger of death.

The doctor and the household servants deem it best to prepare Doña Sales gradually for the return of the prodigal son. Thus, Angel has the whole night to wander through the house and relive his childhood. He tends to excuse his mother for her lack of understanding: "It's a terrible thing that one cannot live with his own feelings, but must accept borrowed ones, those that this stupid bourgeoisie, meddlesome and rule ridden, wishes to impose on us, which wants to govern everything, the state and the family, the group and the individual. . . . I don't blame my mother. . . . I blame the hateful social ambiance in which she has lived and from which she has not been able to escape" (1233b).On the following morning when the confrontation takes place, Angel restrains himself until his mother finally reproves him. His only reaction is to drop her hand which he had been holding. Almost immediately, she goes into her death agony, leaving Angel with a profound feeling of guilt. "Yes, I have to accuse myself, and I shall accuse myself as long as I live of a brutal act. . . . I don't know what happened inside her — everything became unhinged inside her. I would have given my two hands not to have dropped hers." Galdós adds: "This idea tormented him night and day" (1255b).

In Doña Sales's household lived Angel's little daughter Ción and her governess Lorenza, nicknamed Leré. The latter was to play an increasingly important role in Angel's life. Ción was the cause of frequent contacts between the father and the governess. Only a month after Doña Sales's demise Angel is shocked again, by Ción's death. In his loneliness Angel could have turned to Dulce. But his mother's dying wish is that she not be permitted to enter the house, and despite his earlier protest he now argues that "to receive her within those walls would be a grave insult to the memory of the deceased, a sort of posthumous provocation" (1256b). Furthermore he now sees Dulce as a part of her family, even though she is morally far above them. Her brothers and cousins are cheats and counterfeiters, her uncle has been the skipper of a slave ship, her father and mother have pushed her into prostitution. The whole Babel family feels that Angel's new wealth should be shared with them. Although he feels morally responsible to Dulce and does see her occasionally, Angel soon eliminates her from his affections.

We can say, then, that Doña Sales's ideas triumph after her death. Angel certainly cannot accept his mother's social conventionality, even though he subconsciously admits the validity of the charges which middle-class morality brings against him. His idealistic humanitarianism needs a new orientation. In religion and in its advocate, Leré, Guerra finds a new outlet for idealism.

Before his return home, Angel has a low opinion of Leré's worth. "Poor Leré . . . She's a pitiful creature" (1215a), he tells Dulce. She was born in Toledo, the only daughter of a family which produced five "monsters" (four of whom died at birth) and one musical genius, a boy, studying in Belgium on a scholarship at the time of the action of the novel. Leré's own genius is directed toward religion; she wishes to become a nun in a strict nursing order and informs Angel after Ción's death that she will soon leave for Toledo. He gets her to remain another eight days in his home.

Angel's first reaction to Leré is to make her a mother-figure, a surrogate for Doña Sales. She takes over the direction of the servants. While Ción is still alive Angel tells the governess: "The child can't live without you, nor you without her, nor I without the two of you . . . because my mother taught you how to run this house so well that there can be no substitute for you" (1261b). In more intimate details there is also a carry-over from the older woman. Doña Sales was a great believer in "the discipline of the corset" (1244b) which she "did not abandon except when it was impossible to stand it" (1244a). Leré, although she had a good figure and although corsets were not usual in her humble social class, "always wore a corset on the express recommendation of Doña Sales, a strong partisan of a garment which brought with it decency and respectability" (1267b). Even more significant is the fact that Doña Sales had a "bust with massive forms in front" (1244b), and Leré is constantly described as having a "massive bosom" (1232a). When Angel begins to admire her physically it is especially her "massive bosom" (1263b) which attracts him. Conversely, Dulce's flat chest is one reason that Angel rejects her. When he first visits her, six days after Doña Sales's death, he exclaims, "How skinny you are!" and the novelist adds that Guerra thought that "her bosom was no bigger than that of a man" (1263b).

Of course breasts are not just a mother symbol, but also a sex symbol. After Angel has declared his love to Leré, she ponders on the situation. She has no intention of renouncing her religious vocation, but, not without a bit of human vanity, she meditates "there must be something in my person which has pleased him . . . One thing I've never been able to understand is why I have this colossal bosom, if I don't need it. . . . This must be the only part of my body which favors impure thoughts in men. . . . I'd cut it off if one could as one cuts fingernails. . . . [Basilisa, a servant] says that Dulce has a pretty face, but is nothing but skin and bones. . . . I'm sure I didn't become conceited when Basilisa made comparisons between flat chests and others that aren't flat. I, God knows it well . . . would, if I could, go to that woman and say to her 'Let's exchange, friend; take what you need and I have too much of. You will be happy and I will too' " (1294 - 1295b).

When Guerra declares his love to Leré, just before she leaves for Toledo and the convent, his words reveal a mixture of both sexual desire and filial respect. "I love you. . . . What I don't know is how to define the way in which I love you. Do I love you like any other woman? I think not: there is something more, Leré. Your holiness is an obstacle for loving you, and even for telling you about it. And nevertheless your holiness captivates me, and if you weren't as you are, if you didn't have this invincible faith and irresistible vocation, I imagine that I would not like you so much" (1293b). So Angel, separated from Leré by religion as a son is separated from a mother by the incest-taboo, sees the young woman as an unattainable but greatly desired object.

The last two volumes of the novel take place in the intensely religious atmosphere of Toldeo, the mystic city par excellence. Leré enters a nursing order which permits its sisters to receive visitors. Hence Angel is able to see her with a certain regularity and to listen to her advice. She would have him dominate his violent temper and become truly charitable. Finally she urges him to become a priest.

Despite the willingness with which Guerra attempts to put her commands into practice, his old character is never completely submerged. Although he strives to dominate the old impulses and drives by depriving himself of food and sleep, this process only results in dreams and hallucinations, in which the repressed desires find their outlet. Specifically, Angel confesses that one night the sight of Leré sleeping (in a room next to the patient she is nursing) has stirred almost irresistible libidinous passion in him. He dozes off in a chair and later declares that as dawn broke he saw her "surrounded from head to feet with a blinding light; and her eyes looked at me with a severity which made me tremble, and putting her hand to her bosom, she tore off a piece of flesh — it seems to me that I'm seeing it now — a big and very white piece of flesh, dripping blood, and threw it in my face, saying, with more compassion than anger, these

words, which I'll never forget: 'Here . . . for the poor beast' "
(1458a).

A similar hallucination occurs one night when Guerra is lost while
chasing a straying goat down into the deep, rocky chasm of the Tajo
River. In the midst of a violent thunderstorm Angel seems to enter a
lighted cave. There he sees a vision of Leré who gestures for him to
follow her. When Angel tries to embrace her she disappears momen-
tarily and the gentle goat, suddenly transformed into an ugly old
buck, treads on the now prostrate Guerra. When he recovers from a
brief lapse of consciousness he sees Leré throwing flesh from her
breast to the horrible beast and looking at her hapless friend with
pity. He asks her, "Do an evil thought and an instinctive act deserve
such cruel treatment?" (1485). The transparent symbolism of this
hallucination is apparent.

It seems clear now that our protagonist is attracted to Leré both as
a woman and as a surrogate for his deceased mother.[25] We also feel
that Angel wants to obey, and would have gladly obeyed, Doña Sales
in everything had she possessed a more charitable and humanitarian
outlook. As he gets to know Leré her "exalted and ethereal
humanitarianism fascinated him" (1268a). Little by little, obeying
her commands, he becomes a convert to her idealism. Here we must
object to the interpretation of a critic who believes that Guerra
becomes a new and different man after Doña Sales's death.[26] It is
true that Guerra says "I'm not the man I was" (1265a) and that at
times he refers to himself in his earlier political role as "the former
man," but although he becomes religious, his religion is not the one
practiced by 99 percent of the Spaniards; it is a revolutionary force
which would provoke changes even more radical than the political
action with which he is disillusioned. Just as he opposed bourgeois
conventions with revolutionary politics, he now confronts them with
religion.

His grandiose daydream of a new monastic order, open to both
men and women and headed by Leré as prioress, reveals Guerra's intention to break with the reality of both church and society.
Gradually his thinking works up to a climax, at which time he
declares that "works of charity practiced strictly and literally
can bring about a great and true social revolution . . . a beneficent
renovation which politics and philosophy seek in vain" (1513b). The
church does not practice true charity; consequently Angel foresees a
break with Rome and an evangelically oriented independent Spanish
church (1515b).[27] But we should not overlook the comment of Don

Juan Casado, the priest who is Angel's friend and spiritual adviser, and to whom he has been outlining his plan. "If I did not believe that you are speaking without knowing what you're saying, friend Angel, I would think that with all your religious vocation and your mysticism you have not ceased being as revolutionary as when you outdid yourself to alter the established order, before you came to Toledo. However much you change externally . . . there still exists the same old temperament, the distinctive man, always equal to himself" (1515a).

Angel is doomed to failure for two reasons. First, his idealism loses contact with reality; in this case, he forgets that there is evil in human beings, especially in Dulce's brothers and cousin. Then Angel cannot repress his fundamental character. His violent temper breaks out from time to time, as when he almost kills Arístides, one of Dulce's brothers (1379) and again, toward the end of the book, when he reacts angrily to the robbery which Arístides and other recipients of his charity are perpetrating on him (1525b). Policarpo (Dulce's cousin) wounds him fatally; later as he lies dying, nursed by Leré, he tells her in words reminding us of the dying Don Quixote and his renunciation of the dream of chivalry: "It seems to me that I'm waking up now; that this life of mine in Toledo is a dream; that scarcely the space of a night has passed between that time [when we lived] in Madrid and the present moment. My wound, your veil, destroy this illusion. We are no longer what we were then, Leré. . . . [But] I am the one who finds that I'm similar to the one I was then . . . Then I began to love you; afterwards I loved you more and I dreamed of the joy of marrying you . . . The blow which I have received from reality, at the same time that it made me see stars, clarifies my mind and makes it as bright as the sun" (1530b).

His chimera has evaporated, dissolved by the heat of reality. But from Angel's dream one thing does remain: "love, begun as an exclusive and personal feeling, [was] later extended to all humanity, to every needy and helpless being" (1531b). So Angel, now seeing clearly his basically human relationship with the nun, calls her "my wife" (1532b - 1533a), not without a certain gentle humor. The novelist makes him die without having received the sacraments. But a clairvoyant blind woman declares that she "saw" him transported to heaven. Angel is not conventionally religious, but his profound humanism deserves salvation.

In what has been said so far we have skipped over Angel's gradual acceptance of religious idealism, and we must now examine it, particularly because it parallels Galdós's own belief in a number of respects. As soon as Guerra reaches Toledo he enters some of its numerous churches, "moved by artistic dilettantism and by a certain religious curiosity lightly stimulated by yearnings for a spiritual life" (1314b).[28] He is especially aroused by a visit to the convent where Leré had been a student (1316a) but "the atmosphere [of the whole city] was reflected within him most vigorously" (1321b).

Religious music and sculpture (especially holy images) make a deep impression on him (1413 - 14, 1419b) but Guerra questions whether his "eagerness to taste the sweets of piety corresponded to a phenomenon of aesthetic emotion or religious emotion" (1321b). He finds that images of *female* saints help him to pray far more effectively than those of holy men. He becomes particularly devoted to the image of Nuestra Señora del Sagrario, which at times becomes confused with his mental image of Leré (1415a).

The abbess of the nuns who had educated Leré makes a profound impression on Guerra. "It's impossible to describe how striking that lady was. . . . She was a beautiful woman, rather mature, with a majestic bearing, without her beauty and grace detracting anything from the air of a bishop which was given her by her position in the principal chair, her staff, and the manifest subordination of her companions" (1315b). Not long afterward the dream of a new religious foundation, with Leré as its head, begins to take shape (1341b; 1369a; 1372 - 73).

As Angel is now living in his country house *(cigarral)*, across the river from Toledo, the beauty, peace, and repose of the country (1361a) combine with his spiritual yearnings. A sense of well-being, a withdrawal from urban society, and the association with naive, unsophisticated folk lead to his decision to make his country house the nucleous of his foundation. Little by little the idea enlarges and matures until, as we have seen, it is finally a vast revolutionary scheme. Angel finally comes back to reality and recognizes that his grandiose plan is but a sublimation of his physical love.

It should be evident to the reader that Galdós has been probing Angel's subconscious mind, and that he foreshadows ideas which are to appear several years later in Freud and Jung. We must attribute his keen perception of hitherto unplumbed depths to his genius as an observer and creator; not to any technical studies he could have read. He may have developed an interest in psychic phenomena through association with some of his doctor friends, but none of them went beyond a superficial interest in the subconscious.[29]

Certainly Galdós deserves our admiration for his deep insights into Angel Guerra's soul, in which much of his own personality was reflected. Angel's disillusionment with politics and his search for idealism in unconventional religion are undoubtedly based on Don Benito's own experience. Nonetheless, the author's practical common sense tells him that exaggerated idealism is often merely the sublimation of a primordial drive and that in the real world it is doomed to frustration. So Angel, an admirable dreamer, is a failure.

IV   Tristana *and* La loca de la casa *(The Madcap)*

These two minor works appeared in 1892, the year when Galdós saw the dramatic version of *Reality* acted (March 15), in which the critics discovered a strong resemblance to Ibsen's plays (see above, p. 114). It is also the year in which he built his elegant chalet in the outskirts of Santander, incurring heavy expenses that he could not meet. He was to look to the theater as a solution to his financial difficulties.

This statement is supported by the fact that he wrote *The Madcap* [30] in dramatic form and soon afterward (Jan. 16, 1893) presented it on the boards in a slightly abbreviated version. We shall return to this work when we take up Galdós as a dramatist.

Tristana, although not highly considered by Don Benito himself,[31] deserves more attention than it usually gets. The name character is a young woman who wants to live "freely and honorably,"[32] who doesn't want to marry, although she is willing to live with the man she loves (24, 68, 112, and 114), and who wants to find a respectable job and support herself by her own work.

She is in short a feminist, and feminism leads us back to Ibsen, who, by the time of this production, was the author of the moment throughout Europe. But it also recalls Emilia Pardo Bazán, whose campaign for woman's liberation [33] began in 1889, simultaneously with her intimate relationship with Galdós. In essence *Tristana* tells us that however admirable feminist ideals may be, they simply cannot be realized in nineteenth-century Spain. Spanish women of the middle class can aspire only to matrimony or the convent, with a few exceptions such as actresses and courtesans.

Tristana, an orphan, has been left in the care of Don Lope Garrido, an elderly Don Juan who promptly seduces his young charge. He is definitely a man of the past, equated to the *caballeros* of the Golden Age plays (7 and 139) and the figures in Velázquez's *Surrender of Breda* (62). Ultimately the conventional values of the past (Don Lope) engulf the ideals of the future (Tristana).

The young heroine believes there are many ways she can earn a living and gain independence — as an artist, a writer, a teacher of foreign languages, or an organist. She has great talent and makes remarkable progress in most of these careers but soon tires of each one. Her tendency is to idealize each profession (22) and to enjoy it as long as she can dream of triumphal achievement, but she loses interest as soon as practical reality comes into play. She is another example of loss of contact with the real world (24, 93, 107 - 8, 114, 135).

This same attitude prevails in her love affair with a young artist, Horacio. She dreams of living with him, free and equal, without marriage, each one supporting himself through his art. But after Horacio goes to his property on the Mediterranean coast, he becomes more and more indistinct in Tristana's mind. Their past tenderness "was erased from her memory, as Horacio's very person was becoming dim, replaced by an ideal being in whom were summed up all visible and invisible beauties" (114).

An accidental intrusion of reality destroys Tristana's dream life. An infection necessitates the amputation of her right leg, forcing her to realize that the physical body is, after all, a considerable part of a woman's charm. Things of the intellect no longer seem important. She exclaims "I only want good health, even if I am stupid as a dunce" (104). She begins to frequent neighborhood churches, satisfying her "passion for the ideal" by substituting God for the man in whom she had seen the compendium of all perfections (153 - 54).

Don Lope hates matrimony as an institution, but now proposes marriage to Tristana. His relatives have offered him lands in Andalusia with the proviso that he regularize his union with her, and he also feels an obligation to provide for her after his death. To his surprise, Tristana accepts his proposal, as she now feels indifference toward terrestrial things. The marriage takes place; Don Lope develops an interest in gardening and Tristana in cooking. Galdós ends his narrative by asking, "Were they both happy? Perhaps" (157).

The unfinished, inconclusive ending of the novel recalls the final scene of Ibsen's *Doll's House*, where the possibility of Nora's return to Helmer and his treating her as something more than a doll is not ruled out. Furthermore, Tristana is called a "doll" in eight different places in the novel (10, 23, 117, 118, 122, 123, 124, 138). Two years later in the preface to *Los condenados* (The Condemned), Galdós denies being influenced by Ibsen but shows clearly that he had read almost all of the Norwegian master's work.[34] We are left with the suspicion that Tristana's feminism is not unrelated to Nora's.

But if Ibsen's heroine can leave home with a reasonable expectation of making her way in the world, Tristana accepts marriage "as something imposed by the outside world" (156). Galdós is saying that in the Spain of the 1890s reality crushes the dream of woman's independence. Yet he does not reject the ideal for the future. He has Horacio say "Perhaps she [Tristana] sees more than all of us; perhaps her perspicacity, or a certain prophetic instinct conceded to superior women, sees future society which we do not see" (145). However, in the society in which she lives, she must accept the most prosaic lot, the wife of an unloved old man.

V   *The Torquemada Series*

Torquemada, the miserly moneylender, had appeared as a minor figure in *Doctor Centeno, The Bringas Woman,* and *Forbidden Fruit,* besides occupying a somewhat larger place in *Fortunata and Jacinta.* When Galdós gave him the principal role in *Torquemada en la hoguera* (Torquemada in the Fire) he perhaps was already planning the other volumes which he was not to produce until 1893 - 95.[35] In any case other novels and his preoccupation with the theater delayed the completion of the cycle.

The first short volume *(Torquemada in the Fire)* sets the theme for the continuations. Torquemada believes that with his money he can strike a bargain with God; specifically, he believes that he can induce Him to spare the life of his dying son, Valentín. In the final tome, *Torquemada y San Pedro* (Torquemada and Saint Peter), he himself is dying and tries to buy his way into heaven with a huge donation to the church. However, materialism can go only so far. Although Torquemada has climbed to the apex of material well-being, his money is of no value in the realm of the spirit.

In the first volume the miser is a widower, rather indifferent to his daughter Rufina but doting on his twelve-year-old son. Valentín is a mathematical prodigy, whose brilliance astounds his professors. When he falls victim to acute meningitis, his father's anxiety and suffering are immense. Contrary to Torquemada, the Grand Inquisitor, he is the victim, the one seared in the flames.

Most of the afflicted usurer's bizarre ideas on religious matters have been borrowed from his friend José Bailón, a defrocked priest who believes that the real deity is Humanity, the Great Whole.[36] If

Torquemada has been heartless and evil-tempered toward all who borrow or rent from him, how can he expect Humanity to spare his son? In a fit of remorse he rushes out to undo his unfeeling past behavior by a series of charitable acts.

Yet he is never truly charitable. When he meets an old white-haired and bearded beggar, trembling with the cold, he considers giving him his cape, but compromises by running home to get his old cape, keeping the new one for himself. He tries to lend money without interest, an offer which awakes suspicion and is rejected. He gives 3,000 *reales* to Isidora Rufete and her dying artist lover; yet he discounts the sum by two hundred *reales*, saying that he has not the small bills necessary to complete it. He also takes a number of the artist's paintings, declaring he will keep them as mementos, while thinking that their value will surely increase after the painter's death.

Despite Rufina's devoted nursing and the efforts of the doctors, Valentín dies. Torquemada enshrines his memory, framing the blackboard on which the boy's mathematical symbols remain, and later establishing in his room a sort of altar on which he places Valentín's photograph. But convinced that Humanity has not lived up to its side of the bargain, he returns to his harsh, inhuman practices in squeezing the last cent out of his victims.

In *Torquemada en la cruz* (Torquemada on the Cross) we find the miser, now considerably enriched, still grieving for Valentín. He converses with the dead boy's picture and seems to hear replies. As the idea of reincarnation had been preached by Bailón, Torquemada believes that his son wishes to be reincarnated. The miser thinks that if he remarries, Valentín will be born again of the new wife.

The possibility of marriage to a woman of the aristocratic class arises from a recommendation made by Torquemada's old associate in usury, Doña Lupe (see *Fortunata and Jacinta*). At the point of death she urges Torquemada to aid the Aguila family, the last impoverished members of which are two youngish women (Cruz and Fidela) and their blind brother (Rafael). Torquemada does lend them money; Valentín, through his picture, tells him not to charge interest. This generous act gives rise to an invitation to join the family gathering, where Torquemada meets José Ruiz Donoso, a well-bred, cultured gentleman who becomes the miser's ideal. He begins to copy Donoso's speech, dress, and manners, and following his advice, moves from his tenement flat to an apartment of twenty-three rooms in one of the houses he owns. Donoso also insinuates that he should marry. Torquemada makes him his ambassador to seek the hand of one of the Aguila women, and he departs on this mission without knowing whether Cruz or Fidela is the one preferred! Cruz, the stronger, feels it is Fidela's turn to make a sacrifice, and the latter, although not enthused by Torquemada's person, consents as a means of regaining the luxuries and ease which she has been missing. Rigorous opposition comes from Rafael, who detests the idea of mingling the noble Aguila blood with that of a commoner.

Although Rafael wanders off, intending to become a beggar rather than live on Torquemada's money, the marriage does take place, and the blind nobleman, a symbol of the aristocracy's lack of contact with reality, returns to the family. Rafael's story is rounded out in *Torquemada en el purgatorio* (Torquemada in Purgatory), where he feels that his blindness gives him a clairvoyant insight into the future of Fidela's marriage. He is sure that she can never love her husband. But after a son, the second Valentín, is born, he finally realizes that he represents a decrepit, useless, dead past (*O.C.*, V, 1106 - 11). He commits suicide by throwing himself out of a window.

Most of the third volume deals with Torquemada's ever increasing wealth and the manner in which Cruz forces him, much against his will, to increase his expenditures. First he must buy a carriage, then take a box at the opera, and finally buy back the title of Marquis of Saint Eloy once held by a defunct branch of the family. He also becomes a senator and, owing to the construction of a railroad in his district, is acclaimed as its "favorite son." The only way in which he does not prosper is that his son, the new Valentín, is an idiot. The mathematical genius is not reincarnated.

Torquemada and Saint Peter opens in the Palace of Gravelinas, now the possession of our multimillionaire. The palace library includes all sorts of valuable manuscripts, the art gallery displays a fine collection of ancient armor and a magnificent choice of painting. A private chapel, a stable full of horses, numerous servants, and every conceivable luxury exist in Torquemada's new home. But the possessor of all this material wealth is not happy. His wife sickens and dies; his son is scarcely able to speak and becomes physically more and more deformed. Finally, Torquemada himself must face death, as his stomach aches and the inability to hold food warn him of his approaching end.

Meantime the family has come under the influence of Father Gamborena, a priest who had been the chaplain of the Aguila family in his youth and had then spent long years as a missionary in Africa and the Philippines. Now in his old age he has retired to Madrid, where he finds moral corruption rampant. Because the priest looks like the old beggar to whom he gave a cape (in *Torquemada in the Fire*), Torquemada calls him "Saint Peter." He is a positive force for good, especially on Cruz, who renounces much of her aristocratic ambition and devotes herself to charity.

After Torquemada indulges in a gargantuan meal in the tavern of an old friend, he becomes violently ill. Gamborena and Cruz begin to work for the salvation of his soul. She gets him to will one third of his immense wealth to the church; the priest tries to get an expression of sincere repentance from the dying man. But Torquemada becomes befuddled and delirious, constantly muttering phrases about the plan he has devised for the conversion of the external debt of Spain into internal bonds. At the last moment, as Gamborena again exhorts a genuine repentance, Torquemada murmurs "conversion" and dies. The author points out that it is impossible to tell if the word refers to financial or religious matters.

If we were forced to choose between the two possibilities, the conversion of the national debt seems preferable. Torquemada has become a free thinker, proclaiming himself a "scientific man" subject to doubts, not a "poet." He wonders why he should die just when he has thought up a fine scheme of debt conversion which will benefit Spain, the most Catholic nation. He tries to bargain his gift to the church against his personal salvation.

The principal way in which Galdós individualizes the type character of his protagonist is through speech.[37] Especially after he gets to know Donoso he loves to use fancy words and often gives them his own meanings. When he makes a speech at a banquet in his honor (*Torquemada in Purgatory*, part III, chap. 8) he uses all sorts of malapropisms, clichés, and high-sounding phraseology. He provokes laughter and feigned applause; yet when he turns to praise of work as an ethical principle, the ovation becomes sincere. Not everything he says is absurd.

In conclusion, we feel that the Torquemada series suffers mainly by its extreme length. It contains much of Galdós's best writing and humor. Its only fault is that it is too long.

CHAPTER 9

The Triumph of the Spirit

I Nazarín

WE have seen how Galdós put increasing emphasis on forces of the spirit as promoters of human activity. The material stimuli dear to naturalism were gradually giving way to inner drives independent of environment and heredity. Nonetheless, his characters up to this time have not been moved exclusively by the spirit; Angel Guerra, for example, must finally admit that physical desire for Leré underlies his religiosity.

Nazarín, on the contrary, responds exclusively to spiritual compulsion. He is an unconventional, although completely orthodox, priest, whose real name (Nazario Zaharín) gives rise to the nickname linking him with the Nazarene. In fact, Nazarín is a Christ-figure.[1] He follows literally Christ's mandates, which ultimately causes a tribunal to declare him insane. In the modern world a man who loves poverty, who refuses to pass judgment even on criminals, and who will not react in anger to personal insults and offenses is indeed strange. Even Nazarín's fellow priests cannot understand such truly Christian behavior.

The action of the novel is simple: Don Nazario leaves Madrid, barefoot and roughly clad, to wander through villages to the west of the capital. He is joined by two women of the lowest class, Andara,[2] a prostitute that had set fire to the priest's slum tenement and is thus the immediate cause of his leaving Madrid, and Beatriz, an hysterical young woman whose grim hallucinations turn into mystic transports under Nazarín's influence.

A pseudomiracle (the curing of a sick child by prayer and the laying on of hands) enhances the priest's saintly reputation, although he emphatically denies any miraculous powers. The three pilgrims nurse smallpox victims in the villages of Villamanta and Villamantilla. They are robbed, then arrested because of the fire Andara set, and marched back to Madrid under guard, where Nazarín, delirious with a high fever and awaiting the trial which is to declare him insane, has a vision of Jesus. The Lord commends him, saying, "You have done something for me. Do not be unhappy. I know that you are to do much more."

To many other characters of the novel Nazarín is an inexplicable puzzle. In the opening scene, where the narrator and a journalist friend interview Don Nazario in his squalid tenement, the reporter comes away convinced that the priest is a cynical trickster, a parasite scheming to live without working. The narrator does not share this simplistic point of view; he is haunted by Nazarín's unconventional practice of Christianity, and relates the priest's wandering adventures as an attempt to define his true nature. It is not until the sequel *(Halma)* that we learn that society, through the law courts, has judged Nazarín insane, but we already realize that the narrator sees him as a complete Christian.

A number of the plot episodes clearly parallel events in the life of Jesus. Most striking is the scene on the march back to Madrid. Nazarín is shackled between two thieves, one of whom he converts to repentance. Need we point out the similarity to the episode of the crucifixion? Then we note Nazarín's nonresistance to arrest, at which time Andara, like Saint Peter in the Garden of Gethsemane, strikes and wounds slightly one of the arresting officers. We can add Nazarín's love of poverty, to which he aspires as others do to riches, and his disdain for the fruits of modern civilization.

An important episode illustrates this latter point. The mayor of the town in which the pilgrims are arrested prides himself on living in the age of progress, the epoch of the steam engine, the telephone, and the printing press. He tries to convince Nazarín that practical men cannot seriously try to follow literally Jesus's example. Women can immerse themselves in religion but men must seek progress through industry, agriculture, and commerce. To this harangue Nazarín simply replies, "My dear sir, you talk a language I do not understand. The one I speak you don't understand either, at least at present. Let's remain silent" *(O.C.,* V, 1751a).

It is curious to compare Nazarín's attitude toward modern civilization with that of Pepe Rey (in *Doña Perfecta,* chap. 5), who feels that all that is needed for the well-being of Orbajosa is the investment of capital under the direction of intelligent engineers with the assistance of a few thousand workmen. Pepe Rey, with the approval of the author, stands for material progress, a posture Galdós now contradicts in Nazarín.

Besides being a Christ-figure, the wandering priest is also a Don Quixote. Nazarín comes from La Mancha and like Quixote he wants to make his ideal a reality. One specific passage appears to be molded on an episode from Cervantes, although with a reversal of roles. Don Quixote was entertained at the house of the Duke and Duchess where the noble hosts feigned belief in the knight's world of illusions. Nazarín dares to beg food at the manor of the wealthy and irascible Don Pedro de Belmonte, against whom he has been warned. The latter, instead of treating the beggar with his accustomed wrathful cruelty, mistakes Nazarín for an Armenian bishop making an incognito pilgrimage through Spain, about whom the newspapers have been talking. The more Nazarín denies Don Pedro's false identification, the more the deluded host insists on honoring him and ladening him with gifts. The noble, not the Quixote-figure, is mad.

As usual Galdós did not form his protagonist on just one model. Perhaps Ibsen's *Brand,* another personage who took Christ's teachings literally (albeit to the extent of acting with inhumanity toward his family) had something to do with the creation of Nazarín. More probable is the notion that the Catalan poet-priest Jacinto Verdaguer provided Galdós with suggestions. Verdaguer himself thought that Nazarín's situation was identical to his own — persecuted, considered by some a saint, by others insane, living with two women about whom tongues were wagging, and above all, attempting to put Christ's example into practice in his daily life.[3]

Galdós the realist seems to have concluded that things of the spirit are also a part of reality. Undoubtedly very few individuals can live directed only by spiritual forces and in the practical world they quite certainly will not be comprehended. Don Benito realizes that spirituality is easily mistaken for insanity, and that the path of a real-life Nazarín would be strewn with obstacles.

II Halma

Galdós's next novel is an answer to the question of how to bring spirituality into the practical world. Not everyone can be a Nazarín, but all can profit by the example of Catalina, the Countess of Halma, the protagonist of the work named after her.[4] Advised by Nazarín, who plays a secondary role, she makes noninstitutional charity the core of her existence.

The countess was the widow of an impoverished German diplomat whose memory she cherishes as something sacred. Remarriage seems impossible to her. Religion and charity attract her, although she refuses to contribute to the organized charities of aristocratic ladies, thus gaining the reputation of being unbalanced. To carry out her plans she must get control of her paternal inheritance, left in the hands of her Anglophile brother Francisco, the Marquis of Feramor. Galdós paints a humorous portrait of this sober parliamentarian, precise and self-controlled in all his actions, so English in his ways that he is even prematurely bald! Working through a society priest (Manuel Flórez) Catalina persuades her reluctant brother to give her all her heritage and also Pedralba, a dilapidated country estate north of Madrid, which Catalina makes into a rest house or asylum for the poor and broken outcasts of Madrid society.

Among her protégés is José Antonio de Urrea, a cousin of the countess, the possessor of a doubtful reputation because he lives principally on borrowed money. His latest scheme is to found a picture magazine, the first number of which will feature Nazarín and his women companions, now the talk of the town as their trial approaches. Urrea has photographed and interviewed them several times and is convinced of their sincerity, although the aristocrats of Feramor's salon think Nazarín is demented.

Don Manuel Flórez, urged by Catalina, visits Nazarín often and gets the authorities to release him, adjudged insane, under Halma's care and responsibility. Flórez begins to compare himself to Nazarín in whom he recognizes the ideal priest; later, as he sickens and dies, he inveighs against his own life, his aristocratic friendships, and his conventional principles.

When Catalina takes Nazarín and a group of poor people to Pedralba, Urrea follows her. He has come to love her deeply and idealistically. His new life in nature and his healthy outdoor work revive his good qualities. As the notion of making Pedralba into a public asylum gains momentum three local men vie to become its director. Each one feels he is best qualified to head the proposed asylum; yet all agree on one thing, namely that Halma should send Urrea away. Inspired by Feramor, they insist that Urrea only intends to defraud her of her heritage. Halma now seeks Nazarín's advice. He persuades her not to make Pedralba a public institution, which would mean that ecclesiastic and governmental control would take over its direction. Furthermore, he convinces her that the sanctity about which she has been dreaming since the loss of her husband is an affair of her imagination, and that she will never become a true mystic. Finally he shocks her by advising marriage with Urrea.

As she accustoms herself to the idea, she sees that marriage would solve the problem of her charitable foundation. Pedralba would be a private home to which she and her husband could invite anyone they pleased with no interference from outside authorities. Personal charity given without judging the worthiness of the recipient is Catalina's (and presumably Galdós's) idea.[5] Institutionalized charity is often a form of egoism which Galdós had decried as early as *Marianela* and which he will castigate in his next novel, *Misericordia*.

III   Misericordia *(Compassion)*

The power of the spirit to motivate human activity has been the theme of the two novels we have just examined. They are certainly two of Don Benito's finest creations. It hardly seems possible to surpass them, yet that is what he does in *Compassion*.

Nazarín was the exceptional complete Christian, a role to which very few can aspire, and Halma had a sufficient fortune to sustain her charitable plans. What about the ordinary person, who has neither absolute virtue nor money? Can he be so altruistic as to join the ranks of the saints?

Galdós takes a sixty-year-old woman servant as his principal character. Benina has been the maid-of-all-work for Doña Paca for many years, and now when the mistress is penniless, after squandering a fortune on luxuries, clothes, and mundane vanities, the servant is the support of her employer. First she uses all her savings, most of which resulted from her filching a little on all household purchases; then, as the novel opens, she is reduced to begging in the streets or at the church door.[6] Of course she cannot let Doña Paca know the source of her tiny income, so she invents a priest (Don Romualdo) at whose house she is supposed to work during her absences from Paca's barren rooms, all of whose pawnable objects have disappeared.

Benina's charity is by no means limited to her mistress. She shows equal concern for Almudena, a blind Moorish beggar, and for Francisco Ponte Delgado,[7] a gentleman reduced to sleeping in flophouses. On her expeditions into the poorest slums she spends the little money she has buying bread for a clamoring crowd of the desperately poor, some of whom think her Doña Guillermina Pacheco (see *Fortunata and Jacinta*). She must also give material aid to Paca's daughter Obdulia, whose husband does not provide for her.

To satisfy all the demands on her charity she must have money, and begging brings in only a pittance. Since she has run out of credit at the neighborhood shops, her only recourse is to borrow, but from whom? With Almudena's help (pawning his suit) she scrapes together almost a dollar; later she borrows (and pawns) rings from a woman who keeps a low tavern. No sooner does the money come into her hands than it leaves them to appease the most pressing necessities of Doña Paca and the other paupers.

One evening Benina and Almudena are arrested for begging in a prohibited area and confined in San Bernardino, the municipal house of detention. Ironically, this occurs shortly after a real Don Romualdo has tried to call on Doña Paca to inform her of a legacy she is to receive. The suspicious lady, believing him an irate debt collector, has unfortunately not opened her door to him, so Benina must suffer incarceration just when her mistress is once more on easy street.

When Don Romualdo finally gains admission to Doña Paca and Ponte (who also has a share of the legacy) a confusion between the real and the imaginary develops. Is this priest the one Benina talked about? Is the beggar woman named Benina, the associate of a Moor, about whom he tells them a figment of the priest's imagination? After Don Romualdo leaves, Ponte and Paca are almost convinced that he was an hallucination.

The real Don Romualdo returns with monies for the heirs. Paca's daughter Obdulia moves in with her, and Juliana, the daughter-in-law, takes over the direction of the weak-willed Paca's household and finances. She replaces the still-incarcerated Benina with a new servant, her cousin, while Obdulia brings in a second servant, an unnecessary lady's maid, and indulges her passion for flowers by filling the flat with a whole jungle of plants.

Finally Benina and Almudena are released, dirty and ragged, and are turned away from Paca's apartment, owing to Juliana's dominance. After momentary indignation at her mistress's ingratitude, the abandoned servant looks on life with scorn for human vanity (1986b) and can regard Paca's ingratitude without hate or ill will (1987b), certain, as she is, that ingratitude is a universal reaction to charity (1988a).

Meanwhile Ponte, whose mind has become more unbalanced after a fall from a horse, gratefully maintains that Benina is an angel (1989b), another example of "reason from unreason," and finally Juliana seeks out the hut where Benina now lives with the Moor in order to get her assurance that her children will not die. Juliana, the materialist, ends by calling the old woman a saint (1992b).

Galdós himself suggests that Benina is a saint when he gives her the surname "Casia" and compares her to Saint Rita de Cascia (1882b).[8] Although he presents her in a highly naturalistic slum environment, which would certainly influence her toward egotistical self-interest, she is purely altruistic, with the possible exception of her filching from shopping funds, a fault commonly found in Spanish servants. It seems that Galdós did not want to make her saintly to an incredible degree.

Her charity knows no distinctions. When she returns from the house of detention with Almudena she declares that she wants to shelter him in Paca's house just as she had protected Ponte. "If there was compassion for the other man, why isn't there for this one? Or is charity one thing for the gentleman in his frock coat and another thing for the naked pauper? I don't understand it that way" (1982b). By making Almudena, a Moor practicing Judaism, the object of Benina's compassion, the author emphasizes the universality of her charity, for Moors and Jews are usually objects of aversion in Spain.

In 1913 Galdós wrote a preface for the Nelson edition of *Compassion* in which he gives us insights into the origin of this novel. He tells us that he spent "long months" observing and studying from life the poverty-stricken and delinquent types of the low quarters. Accompanied by police or disguising himself as a municipal doctor he visited flophouses and brothels. He had already used the low quarters as background material for large parts of *Fortunata and Jacinta*, and he now tells us that in his documentation for that novel he had encountered prototypes of Benina, Paca, and Ponte. Almudena, however, came to his attention later. A friend drew Don Benito's attention to a Moorish beggar whom Galdós cultivated and copied from life. In *Compassion* he employed the language of the people he had observed, using all their picturesque phrases, some of which he himself did not understand.[9]

What we have just heard about the origins of *Compassion* makes Galdós appear as a strictly naturalistic author, one who makes documentation the heart of his procedure. It is perfectly true that the method is naturalistic, but the new element of spirituality gives quite a different tone to the work.

As in all literary creations something of the author himself enters the aggregate. Most obviously it is Galdós's admiration for the truly charitable protagonist. Perhaps Doña Paca's ingratitude reflects Don

Benito's feelings toward Miguel de la Cámara, from whose partnership he had just separated at the time of writing *Compassion*. Benina's difficulties in acquiring money may be related to the author's own financial straits. *Compassion* is undoubtedly a noble work and one which reveals qualities of the highest order whether judged from the artistic or the moral point of view. Galdós, himself a man of great charity, puts much of his own spirit into the humble but saintly Benina.

IV   El Abuelo *(The Grandfather)*

Galdós wrote this novel in dialogue, like *Reality* and *The Madcap*, probably intending to convert it into a theatrical production and to produce it soon on the stage. However, adverse criticism and a desire to produce the play in Rome caused him to hold off the dramatic production for five years.

The protagonist is the old, impoverished Count of Albrit, who has always thought that family honor is the supreme spiritual force, but who finally discovers that love is far greater. He has two grand-daughters (Nell and Dolly), one of whom is in fact not his son's daughter, as he discovers through letters left by his deceased son. The problem is to find out which girl is the genuine heir of the noble family and which is spurious. Albrit comes to the country town where the girls are living to investigate. Believing that aristocratic blood must reveal itself in noble thoughts and actions, he observes them and questions the local priest, doctor, and teacher about their personalities and conduct. Both have excellent qualities so the count remains in a quandary, preferring first one then the other.

Of course the mother of the two young women, an Irish-American named Lucrecia Richmond, could enlighten him, albeit by admitting her own sinful conduct. Albrit hates Lucrecia; his haughty, autocratic bearing makes her unwilling to cooperate with him in any way until finally, at the insistence of her confessor, she informs him that Dolly's father is a commoner and that the blue blood of Albrit does not flow in her veins.

By this time Lucrecia has decided to take her daughters to Madrid. The lure of social life and a possible marriage to an aristocrat make Nell eager to go with her mother, but Dolly, despite attempts to take her by force, escapes confinement and dedicates herself to caring for her "grandfather." Her spurious origin in no way precludes her love.

Underlying the action of the story is the constant reference to the ingratitude of all those who have benefited from the generosity of Albrit and his ancestors. The enriched peasant couple Venancio and Gregoria, who now own the property where the count was born, soon tire of offering him hospitality. Both the priest and the doctor have been educated at the nobleman's expense. The local town and the nearby monastery of Zaratán owe numerous favors to his family. Yet all conspire to shut Albrit up in Zaratán, for him a virtual prison. Again we see Galdós's hatred of institutionalized charity.

Ingratitude is the opposite of love, and love is of rare occurrence. Besides Dolly, it appears in Don Pío, the girls' old, weak-willed teacher. He is in part a humble, humorous repetition of Albrit for he has six spurious "daughters" who make his life miserable. But he is still naturally good and loving. Although the girls martyrize him and he suffers to the point of contemplating suicide, he still loves them, even though he realizes his foolishness, often saying, "How bad it is to be good!" At the end, Don Pío throws in his lot with the count and Dolly and accompanies them in their exile.

Contemporary critics immediately saw the resemblance between *The Grandfather* and *King Lear*.[10] In fact the two old men have points in common: Lear is mentally deranged, Albrit possessed by a monomania; Lear questions his daughters as to which one loves him most, and Cordelia, although the least eloquent, later proves to be the most loving, while gushing Goneril and Regan are shown to be ingratitude personified. The theme of the bastard opposed to the legitimate child is also in Shakespeare's play in the persons of Edmund and Edgar, but there it is the bastard who is bad and the lawful son who is good. The devotion of Kent to Lear parallels Dolly's self-sacrificing love for Albrit.

Despite the unquestionable influence of the English work, the fundamental problem of Galdós's protagonist is completely different from Shakespeare's. The great common factor is the insistence on ingratitude as a dominant trait of the human condition. Once again we suspect that Galdós is expressing some of his personal feeling about those he had helped in the past, especially his recent partner Miguel de la Cámara. Like Albrit Galdós is now poor, the victim of "money lenders, lawyers, crows and vultures" (*O.C.*, VI, 16a).

Although we can admire the spiritual message of *The Grandfather*, placing love above conventional honor, we do not find that this work lives up to Don Benito's previous novels when examined from the artistic point of view. The dramatic form was a mistake,[11] despite the fact that Galdós defended it in his prologue as the best way of presenting "the spiritual truth" *(O.C.,* VI, 9a). It eliminated — save for material in the stage directions — all descriptions, surely one of Galdós's strongest points. The dialogue drags; the one great question to be resolved, namely, the identity of the legitimate granddaughter, must wait to the final scene, and so to fill out the dimensions of a novel the author introduces much doubtfully relevant matter.[12] It is sad to note the beginnings of deterioration in the great author's work. Pressed by need of money he was probably writing too hastily, as he was soon to do in the resurrected *National Episodes*.

CHAPTER 10

A Sad Decline and End

A LTHOUGH Galdós wrote novels of outstanding merit during the 1890s there are already signs of decline in his creative powers during this decade, particularly in his dramatic works. Later, in the 1900s, there is an ever-increasing weakening accompanied by a deterioration of his physical health and, to some extent, of his personality.

We can trace a growing disposition to resent belittlement and to suspect the motives of those who denied him honors. Throughout his last three decades (1889 - 1920) Galdós's pride was repeatedly wounded by growing opposition to his literary and political stance. He had every reason to consider himself a consecrated novelist and revered champion of liberal ideals; hence his defeat for election to the Royal Spanish Academy (1889) was an eye-opening shock.[1] Although elected unanimously a few months later Galdós postponed taking his seat in the academy for eight years in spite of constant urging by his friends to take his place.[2]

Not long after the rebuff from the academy Galdós was subject to unfriendly, caviling attacks by dramatic critics. His counterattack on the "youngsters of the press" in the prologue of *The Condemned* (1894) shows his mounting irritation with what he considered unjustified disdain for his preeminence. Simultaneously his relations with his partner Cámara were becoming strained, leading to the rupture in 1896.

The common people, especially after his anticlerical *Electra* and his participation in republican (i.e., antimonarchical) politics, apotheosized Don Benito, often calling him a "national glory."[3] Constantly subject to their adulation, it was difficult for Galdós to understand the disdain of the reactionaries and the indifference of the new writers of the Generation of '98.

Next came the protracted campaign to get the Nobel prize for Galdós, which began as early as 1905 with protests that he, rather than Echegaray, should have been the recipient,[4] and lasted up to 1917, when Ramón Pérez de Ayala urged his candidacy.[5] But the prime attempt to win the prize for him came in 1912 — the year he became completely blind — and was frustrated by the reactionary opposition of those who could not forget *Electra*. The chief opponent was the Royal Spanish Academy without whose recommendation the petition was sure to fail.

Then there was an immediate attempt to compensate Galdós for the loss of the Nobel prize by a national subscription.[6] Started by a generous 10,000 peseta donation from King Alfonso XIII, the fund seemed well on the way to reestablish the author's solvency. But many pledges were not paid; Galdós drew against the monies already collected; and finally, when he realized that the fund was being exhausted he turned against Tomás Romero, its treasurer, accusing him of fraud.[7] Galdós threatened a lawsuit but was persuaded to arbitrate by his friends. As Berkowitz says, "thus ended the most pitiful incident in the long life of Benito Pérez Galdós."

The episodes just cited lead us to the conclusion that Galdós suffered from a mild paranoia. Certainly there was a disintegration of his personality, a reaction to the disparagement of his work and to his financial insecurity. We must not think of this antagonism as being merely a matter of his imagination. It was very real; a confidential letter from Juan de Macías asks Galdós for an interview to warn him against persons he thought were his friends.[8] At the heart of his disturbed mental state was the question of money. Galdós never learned how to manage his finances; had he done so his old age might have been a relatively happy one. He would indeed have suffered the loss by death of many family members and friends and the deterioration of his health. There was sadness in store for him in any case; yet it was compounded by extreme poverty.

An immediate result of his growing poverty was his attempt to recoup his fortune by writing, first for the theater, where rewards could be great, and then by reviving the *National Episodes*. Unfortunately he forced himself to produce far too hastily; furthermore, there was a lessening of his inventive powers, which was not noticeable in his earliest dramas but became obvious in both the plays and novels of his last two decades.

I *Galdós and the Theater*

During the 1880s there was a great deal of talk about the decadence of the theater in Spain. It is true that the Spaniards, great patrons of the stage, still attended light comedies and particularly the brief one-act plays that were abundantly produced. What was lacking was the serious drama, similar to the works of Ibsen, Hauptmann, and Maeterlinck, all of whom gained European acclaim in the 1890s.

Galdós himself sent a number of articles to *La Prensa* of Buenos Aires discussing the decadence of the theater.[9] At the same time he realized that the popular French authors Zola and Daudet were dramatizing some of their novels, and he hoped that following their lead might be the source of badly needed funds. As it turned out he was mistaken; his plays by and large did not yield large sums, and they made great inroads on the time that he might have devoted to novels. Not only did he have to attend rehearsals, but he was also constantly urged, and often agreed, to make personal appearances with the traveling actors in Barcelona, Valencia, and other provincial capitals. Cámara, while still his partner, wrote him speaking of Galdós's seeking "new roads that would lead you out of poverty. The first was the theater — the thousands of *duros* (dollars) your staged works were going to earn have apparently materialized only in your imagination."[10]

Of his twenty-two plays, six were dramatizations of novels. The first two (*Reality* and *The Madcap*) were stage versions of novels already in dramatic form. Two later plays (*The Grandfather* and *Casandra*) had also appeared earlier as dialogued novels. We can conclude that the weary, impecunious author sought to maximize the earnings from each composition and, secondly, that he felt insecure about his competence in the structure and techniques of the drama.

There is much evidence to prove this lack of confidence. We know that Galdós got help from Pardo Bazán with the theatrical version of *Reality* and from Echegaray with *The Madcap*.[11] He regularly permitted — even urged — actors to make excisions and alterations in his texts. In an article in *La Prensa* he talks of his inability to prejudge the audience's reaction to a scene, saying that speeches which seemed perfect in rehearsal could produce quite a contrary effect to a packed house. Consequently it is not surprising that Galdós's record of success and failure in the theater is extremely spotty, varying from *Electra*, frantically applauded all over Spain and Spanish America, to *Gerona*, withdrawn from the stage after one performance. In some cases (like *Electra*) success was due to the coincidence of the author's theme with political events which were stimulating popular passions. In another case theatrical critics damned a play *(The Condemned)* after its premiere, causing it to fail on the Madrid stage, although the same work was applauded later in Barcelona.

Clearly, the attention of critics to Galdós's plays far exceeds that given to his novels.[12] The review of the premiere, often with photographs of actresses or of scenes from the play, was a feature of all the newspapers. Galdós feels that the authors of these notices have undue influence and that they are "a grave obstacle for the development of the dramatic art." He flays "the youngsters of the press," to whom editors give the responsibility of judging theatrical productions, admitting that he himself was guilty of the same impertinent criticism in his youth.[13]

We should not forget that another powerful motivation, similar to the spirituality we have seen in the novels of the 1890s, activates much of Galdós's theater. We must not attribute his excursion into drama solely to financial difficulties. He realized that the quickest way to give currency to, and to provoke discussion of, his ideas was to put them on the stage, and, disillusioned with politics, like Angel Guerra, he now sought to regenerate some fundamental national character traits by advocating charity, tolerance, and a breakdown of class barriers. Even his anticlerical plays — *Electra* and *Casandra* — indirectly plead for tolerance by attacking intolerance. Taken as a whole, the plays show Galdós advocating the moral regeneration of his compatriots. He recommends work as a virtue to overcome despair. In two plays an impoverished family of high station is saved by a daughter who establishes a business *(Mariucha* and *Voluntad* [Will Power]). Elsewhere it is by sacrificing personal objectives to the general good that the daughter saves the family by marrying a rich man of low position *(The Madcap)*.

Women are of great importance in most of the plays and they are usually the idealists who carry the author's message. As in earlier works Galdós advocates the intermarriage of upper and lower social classes. It is always the woman of aristocratic birth who makes the decision to take a husband below her rank. The Duchess of San Quintín has lost her fortune, but she does not accept her rich suitor, choosing instead the penniless, illegitimate Victor. Celia, the millionaire heroine of *Celia en los infiernos* (Celia in Hell), wants to marry a poor man *(O.C.,* VI, 1257b) with the idea of bringing about a "social equilibrium" (1275b). Disappointed in her first love, at the end of the play she seems to have found her mate in the young socialist workman Leoncio.

Sympathy for the common people and specifically for political ideals favoring the people run through various plays. Juan Pablo, in *Alma y Vida* (Soul and Life) is the spokesman for the shepherds (972a) who are threatened with dismissal by a heartless overseer. In *Santa Juana de Castilla* (Saint Juana of Castile) Peronuño declares that "the people ought to govern themselves in accord with the sovereign" (1384a). Galdós was always a champion of the humble classes.

It is only natural that the plays should express their author's ideas. While they are not quite thesis plays, there is nonetheless a strong moralizing or didactic element in almost all of them. Galdós extols charity in *El tacaño Salomón* (Stingy Solomon) and humane treatment for the aged in *Pedro Minio*, where he proposes a utopian asylum in which both elderly men and women enjoy such things as a café and a theater and live a full and pleasant life. Again he projects himself into an imaginary utopia in the last act of *Amor y Ciencia* (Love and Learning). Here we enter an ideal institution for caring for deformed or mentally disturbed children.[14]

Several times his message is tolerance of, or even love for one's enemies. *La fiera* (The Wild Beast) deals with cruel enmities of the Carlist War which are finally reconciled by the love of Susana and Berenguer, despite the fact that Berenguer's family has been killed by orders of Susana's father. In *Love and Learning* Dr. Bruno takes back his unfaithful wife and her extramarital child in spite of popular prejudice and his obvious reasons to hate her. Again, in *Saint Juana of Castile*, the author's spokesman advises the Spaniards to fraternize with the hated Flemings (to whom Carlos V has given many sinecures in Spain). "Work together," he says, "in the cultivation of the land and of the arts and you will see how finally the Spanish regions will be rich and happy" (1383b).

More interesting than the conventional morality already observed are the unusual ethical concepts we now examine. The first is the appeal to a higher moral justification for an act which in itself is wrong. Victoria *(The Madcap)* gives a check intended for another person to an impoverished widow, a fraudulent action but on the higher level a noble one (608a). Sor Simona, in the play named for her, saves the life of a young spy by saying that he is her son, using a lie to achieve a good purpose (1351b). The saintly Paternoy and Santamona (in *The Condemned*) both swear solemnly and falsely that the hidden José León is not in the house (758a). Galdós, in his prologue to the drama, states that their false oath is "an act of high charity in which the letter [of the law] has to be overcome by the spirit" (723b). They have recourse to their personal judgment as to what constitutes higher and lower morality, a procedure often open to question.

A number of other characters are victims of mental aberrations, some truly insane, others mildly afflicted. These persons know and speak the truth, as for example the mad Queen Juana, whose ideas on political integration of the people with the royalty (1379b and 1384a) and religious simplicity (1387a) are sane and reflect the author's beliefs. Sor Simona is demented, yet she wants love to overcome hatred (1340b and 1341). Victoria *(The Madcap)* has flashes of mysticism, regarded as a mental weakness, yet her mysticism inspires her generous and noble acts. Pedro Infinito (in *Celia in Hell*) has escaped from the insane asylum and lives in the poorest slums, where he brings happiness to his neighbors by prognosticating future changes in their fortunes. Galdós is again using the device of "la razón de la sinrazón" which we have seen and will see again in a number of his novels.

Galdós's theatrical activities brought him many cordial relations with actors and aficionados of the stage. His correspondence contains numerous letters from the renowned María Guerrero and her husband (and leading man) Fernando Díaz de Mendoza, from Carmen Cobeña, and, late in his life, from Margarita Xirgu. They report on the audience reaction, sometimes suggest changes in plays, and above all ask Don Benito to give them roles in his next productions. Despite some biographers' suggestions to the contrary, there is no hint at anything beyond a friendly professional relationship.

II *The Return to the* National Episodes

After his separation from his partner, to whom he says he owed 82,000 pesetas[15] (more than five times his average annual income), Galdós needed to take drastic measures to recoup his fortunes. Undoubtedly his renewal of the *National Episodes,* which he had sworn to abandon forever, was due to his hope of regaining financial security. He remembered the enthusiastic reception and the profitable sale of the first two series and threw all his energy into duplicating that success with the least possible delay. The Third Series, begun in April, 1898, was finished in October, 1900 — ten volumes in two years and seven months! Unfortunately the new series won only lukewarm critical and popular support, and Galdós was not clear of debt to his dying day.

The third group of *National Episodes* deals with Spanish history from 1834 to 1844, the epoch of the first Carlist War. Don Carlos, brother of the deceased Fernando VII, was next in the male line to the late king, and, by the Salic law which barred women from succession, he had a strong claim to the throne. But Fernando had, after vacillations, left the crown to his infant daughter, Isabel, who had the support of the liberals. The traditionalists, the clerical faction, and the supporters of the local exemptions from national law in the Basque provinces and Catalonia all rallied behind the Pretender. The military action occurred principally in these regions of northern Spain. The best Carlist general, Zumalacárregui, died of a wound suffered in the siege of Bilbao; this city received help in time to turn back the Carlists, after which the defeat of the cause was assured, although the conflict dragged on until ended by a compromise solution, by which all Carlist officers entered the national army with full rank and pay.

The period in question also saw romanticism dominant in Spanish literature, and romantic attitudes were everywhere in life, even in politics. The attempt to kidnap young Isabel II in order to restore her mother as Regent, the plotting of conspiracies in Masonic lodges, the secret missions to confer with enemy officials are historically true. Galdós imbues his fictitious creatures with the same adventurous spirit and makes them partake in passionate loves, dramatic escapes, and coincidental encounters.

The various novels do not have a single unifying character, but Fernando Calpena appears in most of them. He comes to Madrid as a young, classically educated man, a far cry from the romantic hero he soon becomes, as he is protected by an unknown lady who eventually turns out to be his mother, and falls violently in love with Aura Negretti. He constantly refers to Fate as the guiding force of his life. Ultimately Aura, believing Fernando dead, marries Zoilo Arratia, and although she tries later to rejoin her lover, her impending motherhood brings her back to reality. Fernando, for his part, renounces his romantic infatuation with her when he sees her with her child; later he conceives a much more placid and deep-rooted love for Demetria, a girl whom he has gallantly rescued from Carlist territory.

These adventures have a parallel in those of Santiago Ibero, Fernando's friend who loves Demetria's sister Gracia. Thinking himself unworthy of her, Santiago decides he must expiate his sin — an affair with another woman — by becoming a monk. Calpena forces him to go back to Gracia; the two young couples marry and settle near Bordeaux, happy and no longer ambitious, away from the tumult of Spanish politics.

Thus the romantic period comes to an end, in life just as it did in literature. The characters just mentioned achieve a realistic vision of life, reminding us of Lázaro's renunciation of political dreams in *The Golden Fountain*. We know that Galdós did not like romanticism; here he is making fun of it, just as he did in *Torment* (see p. 76).

Two specific novels of the group deserve a moment's attention. Neither one of them includes Calpena or Ibero; hence they are only loosely connected with the Third Series. The first one, *Zumalacárregui*, revolves around an ambivalent priest (José Fago) who is also a soldier, serving first on one side of the conflict, then on the other. He is a highly intuitive person, he acts on presentiments and dreams. He believes himself a great strategist and identifies himself with General Zumalacárregui, whose mind he reads to the point of a transference of ideas. He surmises in advance what the Basque leader is going to do, even knowing intuitively of his approaching death. Fago also dies at the same time as the general.

In his depiction of Fago, Don Benito has loosened his early restraint over his imagination, appropriately enough in a work where romanticism is so prominent. We have to go back to *The Apparition* to find something similar. We find the trend toward parapsychology (transference of thought, precognition) occupying more and more space in later works.

The second independent novel, *La campaña del Maestrazgo* (The Campaign of the Maestrazgo), has Don Beltrán, an elderly nobleman impoverished because of his great generosity, as its protagonist. Captured by the Carlist General Cabrera, he witnesses barbarous acts of cruelty and narrowly escapes execution. Word reaches his family that he has in fact been killed. A sumptuous funeral service is held. Don Beltrán, like Don Juan Tenorio in Zorrilla's play, has survived his own "death."[16] Another reminiscence of a romantic situation appears in the same novel. The young soldier Nelet desperately loves Marcela[17] but cannot marry her because he has killed her brother and because she is a nun.

Throughout the Third Series there are many comparisons of real-life events to the theater. The Carlist War is a drama *(O.C.,* II, 1035) with a weak denouement; the claims and activities of the opposed branches of the royal family are a farce (1081a); the outcome of Calpena's love for Aura Negretti is the final scene of a play (902a, 909b). Galdós, recently devoted to the theater, sees events in dramatic terms and implies that the people of the romantic period are acting parts, living in a world of unreality. So although he gives rein to his imagination he disapproves, as always, of letting the dream submerge reality.

There are autobiographical hints in several novels. Bravo Carrasco, relatively wealthy in his country home, finds himself in straitened circumstances in Madrid. He was obliged to contract debts because of favoring needy relatives (O.C., II, 1321b). He had to borrow at usurious rates (1323a) and soon lost any "clear notion of his finances, not knowing what he was spending and what he possessed" (1339b). Galdós could have taken these details from his own life. A less precise parallelism exists between the author and Don Beltrán Urdaneta. This elderly gentleman, who has wasted his patrimony and is now losing his sight, opened his purse to all petitioners and always had pennies for children (696b) and cigars for the men (697a). Although his stingy grandson keeps him on a tiny allowance, Don Beltrán borrows money to indulge himself in his noble generosity (698b and 703b). If this is not a direct reflection of Galdós's openhandedness, it is at least a statement of his ideal.

The Fourth Series of *National Episodes* (written between March, 1902, and May, 1907, a period in which Galdós also produced five dramas) covers historical events from 1847, shortly after Queen Isabel II's marriage, to the revolution of September, 1868, when she was deposed. Her reign was an epoch of moral laxity, the tone of which was set by the queen herself, who bore nine children despite her husband's impotence. Politically most of the reign was dominated by Narváez, in all but name a dictator. The upper classes, enriched by growing industrialism and their buying of confiscated church properties, took no interest in good government; the army continually interfered with, or even overthrew, the ministries, of which there were about sixty during the two decades covered by the Fourth Series. Galdós views the failure of political and social progress as the thwarting of the plans of a few liberty-loving individuals by an oppressive, corrupt society.

Of course not all those who start out cursing the establishment remain true to their ideals. José Fajardo, the protagonist and narrator of the first two volumes of the series, succumbs to bourgeois-capitalist temptations and marries an extremely fat but very rich woman, becomes a deputy in the parliament, and receives a title of nobility. Lucila Ansúrez, after losing the man of her romantic dreams, settles for marriage to the elderly widower Vicente

Halconero, a well-to-do farmer. Both Fajardo and Lucila discover many virtues in their spouses, yet both have relinquished their original rebelliousness against social immorality.[18]

Other principal characters maintain their hostility to debased society. Virginia Socobio left her handsome (although rather effeminate), well educated, upper-middle-class husband and eloped with Leoncio Ansúrez, a manly revolutionary of the common people. Together they hoped for a social regeneration through the revolution of 1854; its disappointing outcome caused them to flee Madrid. In spite of numerous hardships Virginia's life with Leoncio becomes one of self-fulfillment, happiness, and true, albeit unconventional, morality.

Teresita Villaescusa is another rebel. Of a middle-class family, seemingly indifferent to men, and headed for the convent, she changed into a cocotte, a sort of female Robin Hood, taking from her numerous rich lovers and giving to the unfortunate. Her heart does not go out to any of her victims, although she treats them fairly and with a sort of maternal consideration. Not until she meets Santiaguito Ibero (son of Santiago Ibero of the Third Series), does she fall in love. Ibero, many of whose experiences reflect those of the author,[19] is a disillusioned idealist who winds up in self-imposed exile with Teresita.

A historical personage, the priest Martín Merino who tried to assassinate Isabel II, embodies Galdós's judgment of the queen's reign. Don Benito was no friend of regicides; still he believes that Merino was the instrument of a moral law higher than man-made rules, an attitude we saw in the dramas *The Condemned* and *The Madcap*. The would-be assassin receives a sympathetic treatment from the author.

There is no single unifying protagonist running through the volumes of the Fourth Series. Some cohesion is achieved through making several of the leading characters members of the same Ansúrez family. They first appear living like gypsies in the ruined castle of Atienza, where Jerónimo, the father, has taken his children as a protest against the government that did not let him make a living as a farmer because of the multitude of taxes and regulations (*O.C.*, III, 1521b). Through a man (Miedes) learned in local history, Galdós brings out the historical importance, even in the remote ages, of Atienza; thus he makes the Ansúrez family the living continuation of the ancient Celtiberians, or the quintessence of Spanish nationality. Their miserable condition, the result of incompetent government,

symbolizes the generally deplorable state of all Spaniards of the peasant and laboring classes.[20]

Galdós makes Fajardo into an amateur historian who keeps a diary
recording for future generations the events of his time. He engages
the services of Santiuste as his reporter on the Spanish expedition
into Morocco and the attempted invasion of the Carlists at La
Rápita. Santiuste becomes a significant conduit of Don Benito's
thought when he rewrites the history of nineteenth-century Spain,
his *Logical-Natural History of the Spaniards*.[21] Logically, he says,
the Cortes should have had both Fernando VII and Don Carlos ex-
ecuted, thus avoiding the predominance of the clerical party and the
divisive Carlist Wars. Santiuste takes his "history" seriously; obviously he is mad and eventually goes to the insane asylum. Galdós
treats him in a humorous fashion while admitting that Spain would
be far more happy and democratic if these mad ideas had become
reality. As Teresita Villaescusa says, "the reason of unreason is
sometimes the supreme reason" (*O.C.*, III, 722), or to paraphrase
her words, madmen sometimes have the right idea. History as it
might have been contrasts with the corrupt reality which Galdós ex-
coriates throughout the Fourth Series.

The last novels of the Fourth and all of the Fifth Series cover
events after their author had arrived in Madrid and which in many
cases he observed personally. We have noted that Santiaguito Ibero
shares many common experiences with Don Benito. In the Fifth
Series Vicente Halconero (the younger) continues the role by incor-
porating some of the author's activities in his own.

The last, incomplete Fifth Series of *National Episodes* covers the
period 1868 to 1880. Its leading thread is the failure of the ideals of
the Revolution of '68 and its tone is satirical. Galdós was disillusioned by Spain's inability to shake off the bonds of tradition;
probably he also viewed his own life with less than complete approval as he made his semiautobiographical projection (Vicente
Halconero) a mediocre man, always a failure. The series falls into
two distinct parts. The first two volumes continue in much the same
manner as previous episodes, but the last four bring in an element of
magic and fantasy quite incongruous with the realism Galdós
formerly professed.

The narrator of the last volumes is Tito Liviano, a name
suggesting a frivolous and lewd historian.[22] At times the author
changes Tito's name to Proteo Liviano, for this fantastic creature has
a way of shifting magically from place to place, of becoming invisi-

ble, and of entering unperceived even such secret places as the
king's bedroom. Like Fago (see above, p. 147) he can project his
thoughts into, or receive telepathic messages from, other men's
minds (*O.C.*, III, 1313a). He also lives up to the lewdness implied in
his name by his numerous and indiscriminate conquests.[23] Tito
collects historical evidence for Clio (or Mariclío) in a relationship like
that of Santiuste to Fajardo. The muse of history (Clio) appears in
different guise (sometimes old, sometimes young) at important
historical events, but she depends on Tito for reports on the insignificant occurrences that give the tone of the epoch.

In the last episode Galdós has Tito condemn not only the political
system of the Restoration but also revolutionary movements. "The
Spain which aspires to a radical and violent change in politics is
becoming in my opinion as anemic as the other [party]. Years . . .
perhaps more than half a century must pass before this regime, suffering from ethnic tuberculosis, will be replaced by another which
will bring in new blood and luminous ideas" (*O.C.*, III, 1363).
Profoundly disillusioned by the past stagnation of Spain and his disappointed hope for some concrete results from the republican movement, Galdós can still close the final episode with cautious optimism
and the same advice he gave his compatriots in his earliest novels,
namely, wait for the propitious time, and work for change but avoid
revolutions which are often counterproductive.

III *Last Novels*

The element of the marvelous and the mythic that dominates the
last four episodes also pervades *El caballero encantado* (The
Enchanted Gentleman) and *La Razón de la Sinrazón* (The Reason of
Unreason). Both of these late novels are allegories intended to convey a message to the Spaniards. In a sense they are a farewell from a
man who realizes that nothing can be done in his times; only the
cultivation of virtues can bring a future utopian state.

The Enchanted Gentleman involves a hardhearted landowner
who is completely insensitive to the sufferings of the workers on his
estates. He is magically transformed into a peasant, and, seeking
work, he wanders through the heartland of the Celtiberians, including Atienza (where we met the Ansúrez family) and Numancia,
the ruins of the city which preferred destruction to surrender to the
Romans. A mythic figure, the Mother, advises and directs his life.
She is a combination of the Earth Mother and the Motherland. At
last the protagonist is returned to his former state, not without hav-

ing abandoned his old cruel indifference toward the hardships of the
peasants.

The Enchanted Gentleman (1909) precedes the last four *National
Episodes* and anticipates their use of magic. *The Reason of Unreason*
(1915) comes later and is Galdós's last novel. Alejandro, its
protagonist, has lost a fortune owing to his inability to manage his
finances and his scrupulous honesty. He realizes that success in
business depends on lying and that right and justice must yield to
evil. So he gets a diabolical magician to make his untruths become
true. However Atenaida, a woman who symbolizes Reason and
Truth, continues to urge him to renounce "realities" fabricated from
unreality. Finally they flee from an earthquake and fire that destroy
the city and settle in the country where Alejandro cultivates the soil
and Atenaida, a teacher, cultivates the minds of the children of the
region.

Galdós urges a return to fundamentals, work — which he calls
"the true virtue" — (*O.C.*, VI, 395b) applied to the "fertile physical
and spiritual fields" (*ibid.*, 400a).

IV *Weakened Creativity and Health*

We must now face the question if there was in fact a falling-off of
Don Benito's literary powers during the twentieth century and even
in many of his dramas of the last decade of the preceding century.
Some critics have seen his resort to magical plots and characters as an
attempt to renew and modernize his fountains of inspiration;[24]
others believe he achieved a position of extemporality which placed
him on an "ironic Mount Olympus";[25] still others detect the beginnings of senility. For us there is no doubt that hasty composition is
the constant that is observable in all these late works. Galdós could
write more quickly by using ready-made mythological characters
and set figures from literary tradition — Don Juan, Juan Ruiz, Don
Quixote[26] — than by inventing wholly new personages. He had
perhaps already depicted all the possible types he had known and
was forced to repeat them.[27] In any case his inventiveness shows a
sharp decline and unlike many characters in his earlier works, no one
character in his twentieth-century production stands out as an im-
perishable creation. There is also a considerable repetition of
thematic material.

If haste was the proximate cause of Don Benito's literary decline
the underlying cause was his poverty. Letters to his lawyer, the
famous politician Antonio Maura, show Galdós optimistic in 1898
about his new enterprise of publishing his own works, although

burdened by crushing debts. He was forced to postpone payments owed to Maura, and to continue the *National Episodes* even though he hoped to take a long rest before finishing the Third Series.[28] In fact he declared that he would write no more *Episodes* once he finished the Third Series, and again he intended to stop after the first two volumes of Series Five. But he was always compelled to continue them.[29]

The phenomenal success of *Electra* brought some relief but did not permit the liquidation of all of Don Benito's debts.[30] In 1913 documents show him owing 15,000 pesetas on one loan and requesting its increase to 25,000 pesetas. His request was denied, although he did get an additional 1,500 pesetas due to the strenuous efforts of one of his friends.[31] Finally, in his last years, Galdós's lawyer (José Alcuín) allotted the author 200 pesetas a month, which we see him using for tobacco, nightshirts, and generous New Year gifts to servants.[32]

Along with his burden of debts, due in part to his excursion into antimonarchical politics (1907 - 1914), Galdó suffered also from worsening health. Even as early as the beginning of the century he was afflicted by arteriosclerosis[33] followed by a hemiplegic stroke in 1905.[34] In a letter (dated July 31, 1906) recently acquired by the Casa-Museo Pérez Galdós he writes, "You probably know already that I have eye trouble for which they are going to operate."[35] This first operation did not relieve the pain in his eyes and temples; he had to dictate part of *Amadeo I* (fall of 1910) and underwent a second operation on his left eye (May, 1911) and finally a third one on his right eye (April, 1912).[36] The sad result was blindness.

In spite of his afflictions Galdós gave in to appeals from the antimonarchical forces and occupied a place on the platform during political rallies. He was the honorary head of the Republican-Socialist Coalition which brought down the ministry of his former friend and lawyer Antonio Maura after the tragic week of antiwar demonstrations in Barcelona. Later he came to be a symbol of the aspirations of the workers. The blind novelist appeared at meetings under pressure from politicians who used him as a kind of banner to rally popular support.

These activities cost Galdós the support of the academy (headed by Maura) and the loss of the Nobel prize as well as contributions of the rich and powerful to the national subscription. The workers' empty purses could not back their enthusiasm for "the grandfather" (as they nicknamed Galdós). "A halo of respect and admiration of the common people surrounded him"; yet when his statue in the

Retiro Park was unveiled one year before his death very few prominent national figures were present.[37] Galdós had outlived himself; isolated from the mainstreams of national life, his chief consolation was the faithful care of his servants and the love he inspired in children and dogs. Only a few friends continued to visit him.

When death came from uremia (January 4, 1920) Galdós suddenly passed from near oblivion to front-page prominence. His body lay in state in the City Hall where some thirty thousand persons did him homage. The procession to the cemetery drew a multitude of ordinary, poor people who were burying the champion of their rights. Liberal newspapers extolled the deceased; reactionary and Carlist-oriented papers abused him. This political division of opinion lost sight of the fact that Galdós was not really a politician. "In fact the principal traits of his character are the reverse of those qualities peculiar to politicians. As the *Universal Daily* was to recall, his work 'was nothing but a constant call and continuous invitation to tolerance, peace, and brotherly love.' "[38]

V *In Conclusion*

It has been our intention to put the facts of Galdós's life and writings in a new focus with the hope of gaining a deeper and more accurate insight into the great novelist's true personality. We have sought out new data in letters and documents only recently available, and we have tried to clear away myths that Don Benito himself was too reticent to destroy. One example is the false belief that Galdós had very few interpersonal relationships with either family or friends; another is the myth that he was interested in women only to indulge an extremely powerful libidinous nature.

Against these erroneous ideas we have brought forward his deep familial involvement and wide-ranging charity, as well as the tenderness with which he provided for Lorenza Cobián and their daughter, which concerns did much to impoverish the author. Surely Don Benito was a warmer and much more loving person than has been hitherto realized.

At the time of his death the tide of his literary fame was at low ebb but since then it has been steadily mounting. With the perspective of the years attention is now focused on his great novels, such as *Fortunata and Jacinta* and *Compassion*, and at present all agree that he deserves to be ranked among the most talented and outstanding of the nineteenth-century novelists. In Spanish literature only Cervantes outranks him.

Notes and References

Chapter One

For considerations of space, books named in the Notes and References that appear in the Bibliography usually have no publisher, place, and date of publication indicated.

1. G. Marañón, *Efemérides*, p. 45.
2. Manuel Ugarte, *Visiones de España*, p. 94.
3. Sebastián de la Nuez y José Schraibman, *Cartas del archivo de Galdós*, p. 196.
4. Marañón, *op. cit.*, pp. 47 and 45.
5. H. Chonon Berkowitz, *Pérez Galdós, Spanish Liberal Crusader*, p. 250
6. Ugarte, *op. cit.*, p. 94.
7. Gregorio Marañón, *Toledo*, p. 155.
8. Berkowitz, *op. cit.*, p. 302.
9. Ruth Schmidt, *Cartas entre dos amigos del teatro, M. Tolosa Latour, Benito Pérez Galdós, passim.*
10. G. Marañón, *Tiempo viejo y tiempo nuevo* (Madrid: Espasa-Calpe, 1947), p. 96.
11. "Affectionate sisters free him from domestic cares and surround him with the love which his childish soul needs." Kasabal, in *El Nuevo Mundo*, Feb. 1, 1894.
12. A. Armas Ayala, "Galdós, editor," *Asomante* 19 (1963), 45 and 39.
13. Quoted by Carbarga in *Boletín de la Biblioteca Menéndez Pelayo*, XXXVI, 384.
14. Marañón, *Toledo*, pp. 151 and 154.
15. Berkowitz, "Gleanings from Galdós' Correspondence," *Hispania* 3 (1935), 289 - 90.
16. Marañón, *Toledo*, pp. 161 and 170.
17. M. Menéndez y Pelayo, *Heterodoxos*, ed. Artigas (Santander: CSIC, 1940 - 59), VII, 486 - 87. He adds that Galdós is also "a gentle and honorable man."

18. Menéndez y Pelayo, *Discursos leídos en la R. Academia* (Madrid, 1897), p. 75.

19. C. Bravo Villasante, "28 cartas de Galdós a Pereda", *Cuadernos Hispanoamericanos*, no. 250 (October 1970), 19.

20. Benito Pérez Galdós, *Discursos*, pp. 154 - 55.

21. C. Bravo Villasante, *op. cit.*, pp. 25 and 23.

22. Benito Pérez Galdós, *op. cit.*, pp. 153 - 54.

23. Berkowitz, *Pérez Galdós, Spanish Liberal Crusader*, p. 419.

24. See *Excelsior* (Mexico City), Nov. 14, 1971, and Pattison, "Two Women in the Life of Galdós", *Anales Galdosianos* 8 (1973), pp. 23 - 31. For another recently revealed love affair, see A. F. Lambert, "Galdós and Concha-Ruth Morell," *Anales Galdosianos* 8 (1973), pp. 33 - 49.

25. Berkowitz, *op. cit.*, p. 437; *Hoy* (newspaper), Jan. 9, 1920.

26. "El Bachiller Corchuelo," in *Por esos mundos* 11 (1910), 41.

27. Angel Martín (Galdós's coachman in 1917), in *Excelsior* (Mexico City), Nov. 11, 1917.

28. Such as the woman who insulted Galdós in the street; see Luis de Oteyza, *López de Ayala*, p. 178 ff.

29. Berkowitz, *op. cit.*, p. 328.

30. The second part of *Angel Guerra* is dated "Santander, diciembre 1890"; the third part "Santander, mayo de 1891." María Galdós herself told me that Santander was her birthplace. Although the plaque placed by Galdós's admirers on the house in Toledo where the author usually stayed states that "here he wrote . . . *Angel Guerra*," Galdós's letters to Navarro Ledesma tell a different story. On Jan. 16, 1891, he asks Navarro many questions about Toledan topography, and says he will make a flying trip to Madrid and Toledo in February. Another letter (Feb. 8) says he will leave for Toledo in ten days. He spent only a week there. Carmen Zulueta, *Navarro Ledesma*, pp. 281 - 83, 326.

31. *La sombra*, ed. Cardona, p. 55.

32. A good example of such an incorrect assumption is the report of an affair with Juanita Lund, quite untrue. See *Anales Galdosianos* 2 (1967), 139

33. J. Casalduero, in *Hispania* 53 (1970), 828 - 35, comes to much the same conclusion as expressed here. In *La de Bringas* Don Benito, apparently voicing his own conviction, says " . . . it is very unusual to find two persons in complete adjustment and understanding within the cage of matrimony" *Obras completas*, Aguilar (hereafter *O.C.*), IV, 1588b.

On the other hand, the promiscuous men who appear in many Galdosian novels do not have the author's approval. Joaquín Pez and Sánchez Botín of *The Disinherited Woman*, Manuel Pez in *The Bringas Woman*, José María Bueno de Guzmán *(Forbidden Fruit)*, Juanito Santa Cruz *(Fortunata)*, and many others are objects of disdain. Not until we reach *Reality* (1889) do we find an illicit love treated sympathetically, and this work coincides with Don Benito's own affairs with Pardo Bazán and possibly with Lorenza Cobián

Chapter Two

1. Berkowitz, *Pérez Galdós, Spanish Liberal Crusader*, p. 5.

2. Berkowitz, *op. cit.*, p. 19; D. F. Brown in *Hispania* 39 (1956), 403.

3. For an account of Don Sebastián's trip to Paris to help Doña Dolores's exiled brother, see Pedro Ortiz Armengol, in *Estafeta Literaria*, July 1, 1967.

4. It is often stated that there were five boys and five girls, an example of the many small errors in Galdós's biography. Documents in the Casa-Museo Pérez Galdós show clearly that the division was four and six.

5. El Bachiller Corchuelo, in *Por esos mundos* 11 (1910), 45.

6. Berkowitz, *op. cit.*, p. 33.

7. M. Guimerá Peraza, *Maura y Galdós* (Las Palmas: Excmo. Cabildo de Gran Canaria, 1967), p. 19.

8. C. Zulueta, *Navarro Ledesma*, p. 324.

9. *O.C.*, VI, 933.

10. L. y A. Millares Cubas, in *La Lectura* 20 (1919), 346.

11. Reproduced in Berkowitz, *op. cit.*, p. 464.

12. J. Schraibman, "Galdós, colaborador de *El Omnibus*" in *Anuario de Estudios Atlánticos*, no. 9 (1963), pp. 289 - 92.

13. Berkowitz, "The Youthful Writings of Pérez Galdós" in *Hispanic Review* 1 (1933), 91, and J. Pérez Vidal, *Galdós en Canarias*, pp. 90 - 130.

14. See Ernesto Moreno, *Influencia de los sainetes de Don Ramón de la Cruz en las primeras obras de Benito Pérez Galdós* (Ph. D. diss, University of Minnesota, 1966).

15. *O.C.*, VI, 1563.

16. Galdós's essay on Castro, *El Correo de España*, Feb. 13, 1871.

17. See Galdós's essay on Camús, *O.C.*, VI, 1623 - 25.

18. Published in *La Nación*, Jan. 26, 1868, and in *El Correo de España*, July 28, 1871.

19. J. Blanquat, "Lecturas de juventud," in *Cuadernos Hispano-americanos*, nos. 250 - 52 (Oct., 1970 - Jan., 1971), 161 - 220, and W. Pattison, *B. P. Galdós and the Creative Process*, pp. 7 - 16.

20. *O.C.*, VI, 1559.

21. See *Madrid en sus diarios*, III, 350 ff.

22. *Ibid.*, p. 357.

23. L. Antón de Olmet y A. García Carraffa, *Los grandes españoles — Galdós* (Madrid: Alrededor del Mundo, 1912), p. 65.

24. An allusion to the shabby locale of the old Atheneum.

25. *O.C.*, VI, 1560.

26. *Ibid.*, 1730.

27. *Ibid.*

28. *Fortunata . . .* , part III, chap. 1.

29. Berkowitz, *B. Pérez Galdós, Spanish Liberal Crusader*, p. 53.

30. *O.C.*, VI, 1730.

31. In the essay on Dickens, published in *La Nación*, March 9, 1868.

32. *O.C.*, VI, 1730.

33. *O.C.*, VI, 1731 - 32.

Chapter Three

1. *Las Novedades*, Oct. 2, 1868, and *La Nación*, Jan. 2, 1868.

2. See A. Linares Rivas in *El Constitucional*, May 14, 1878, and J. Ferreras in *La Ilustración de Madrid* 2 (1871), 359 - 62.

3. William H. Shoemaker, "Galdós y *La Nación*," in *Hispanófilo*, no. 25 (1965), pp. 21 - 50, studies and catalogues Galdós's articles. His edition of the complete collection *(Los artículos de Galdós en "La Nación")* has been published recently (Madrid: *Insula*, 1972).

4. Antón de Olmet y García Carraffa, *Los grandes españoles — Galdós* (Madrid: Alrededor del Mundo, 1912), p. 37.

5. See Pattison, *Galdós and the Creative Process*, pp. 22 - 23.

6. Published with a perceptive introduction by W. H. Shoemaker, *La Crónica de la Quincena*, (Princeton, 1948).

7. *La Guirnalda*, Jan. 1, 1874.

8. A. Armas Ayala, "Galdós y sus cartas," *Papeles de Son Armadans* 40 (1966), 26 and 29 - 30.

9. Most of these articles were republished by A. Ghiraldo in the first seven volumes of the *Obras inéditas* of Galdós.

10. See Julio Nombela, *Obras literarias*, vol. IV, *Proemio*.

11. Galdós, "Revista de la Semana," *La Nación*, May 24, 1868. Ramón Mesonero Romanos was a respected older writer, a master of the familiar essay on social types and Madrid customs. Galdós admired and respected him; he in his turn admired Benito's early novels and aided him with recollections of the events of his boyhood, which were the background of Galdós's historical novels. See E. Varela Hervías, *Cartas de Pérez Galdós a Mesonero Romanos* (Madrid, 1943).

12. Juan Pló, "El periodismo en Madrid," *El Diario del Pueblo*, May 5, 1872.

13. Galdós, "Observaciones sobre la novela contemporánea en España," *Revista de España* 15 (1870), 163.

14. Shoemaker, *Crónica de la Quincena* (Princeton: Univ. Press, 1948), pp. 35 - 37.

15. It had been published serially in the *Revista de España* (May - Dec., 1871) and in *El Debate* (Dec. 5 - 21, 1871).

16. *La Sombra*, ed. of 1890, prologue. Reprinted in W. H. Shoemaker, *Los prólogos de Galdós* (Mexico, 1862), pp. 67 - 68.

17. Edition of R. Cardona, pp. 37 - 38. Subsequent page references in the text are to this edition.

18. Galdós says that Anselmo's laboratory was like "those which we have seen in more than one novel" *(ibid.*, p. 4). It recalls vaguely Dickens's *Old*

Curiosity Shop. See also the description (that appeared soon afterward) of a scientific laboratory in Pardo Bazán's *Pascual López,* chap. 8, and the astronomical observatory in Alarcón's *El escándalo,* book VII, chap. 5, both of which emphasize the weird, gloomy, and mysterious.

19. As suggested by Cardona, *op. cit.,* p. xviii.

20. See Rafael Bosch, *"La Sombra* y la psicopatología de Galdós" in *Anales Galdosianos* 6 (1971), 21 - 42. For an attempt to interpret the novelette as an allegory, see J. Casalduero, "La Sombra", in *Anales Galdosianos* 1 (1966), 33 - 38.

21. Harriet S. Turner, "Rhetoric in *La Sombra*" in *Anales Galdosianos* 6 (1971), 5 - 19.

22. See Dorothy S. Rundorff, *Spaniards' Lack of Contact with Reality as it is Illustrated in the Characters of the Novels of Benito Pérez Galdós* (M.A. thesis, University of Minnesota, 1950).

23. B. P. G., "Observaciones sobre la novela contemporánea en España," *Revista de España* 15 (1870), 163.

24. *La fontana de oro,* in *O.C.,* IV, 36. Page references in the text refer to this edition.

25. The first edition of the novel had a different ending: Elías pursued the lovers and fatally wounded Lázaro; Clara died from the shock and grief. See Joaquín Gimeno Casalduero,, "Una novela de dos enlaces," *Ateneo,* no. 88 (Sept. 15, 1955), pp. 6 - 8.

26. See Juan López-Morillas, "La fontana de oro," *Revista Hispánica Moderna* 30 (1965), 273 ff.

27. Elías is like an owl (15); two of the Porreño sisters, a panther and a seal (176).

28. An *abate* is a man who has taken minor orders and receives income from a church benefice. He has no ecclesiastical duties and traditionally is a society gossip or busybody.

29. The *manolo* is a dandy of the lower classes of Madrid.

30. *El audaz,* pp. 238, 242. See E. Moreno, *op. cit.,* chap. 2, n. 15.

Chapter Four

1. B. P. G., "Observaciones sobre la novela contemporánea en España," *Revista de España* 15 (1870), 167.

2. *La de San Quintín,* act 2, scenes 9 and ff.

3. In *Torquemada en la cruz* and *Realidad.*

4. *Discursos leídos en la Real Academia Española,* pp. 18 - 19.

5. *El 19 de marzo y el dos de mayo* shows both aspects of the common people. See Matilde Carranza, *El pueblo visto a través de los "Episodios Nacionales"* (San José de Costa Rica, 1942).

6. Interview with Viator, published by J. Blanquat, "Au temps d' Electra," *Bulletin Hispanique* 68 (1966), 304 - 08.

7. S. Ortega, *Cartas a Galdós,* 415 ff.; G. Cheyne, "From Galdós to Costa

in 1901," *Anales Galdosianos* 3 (1968), 94 - 98; J. Blanquat, "Documentos galdosianos: 1912," *ibid.*, 143 - 50; and Clara Lida, "Galdós y los *Episodios Nacionales*," *ibid.*, 61 - 77.

8. See V. Lloréns, "Galdós y la burguesía," *Anales Galdosianos* 3 (1968), 51 - 59.

9. See A. Regalado García, *B. P. G. y la novela histórica española* (Madrid 1966), especially pp. 102 ff.; answered by R. Carr in *Anales Galdosianos* 3 (1968), 185 - 89, and Peter B. Goldman, *ibid.*, 6 (1971), 113 - 24.

10. Alfred Rodríguez, *An Introduction to the "Episodios Nacionales,"* p. 42.

11. *Mendizábal*, *O.C.*, II, 435.

12. *Zumalacárregui*, *O.C.*, II, 424. See Hans Hinterhäuser, *Los "Episodios Nacionales" de Benito Pérez Galdós*, pp. 120 - 21.

13. In the seventeen years of his association with Cámara, Galdós earned 242,632 pesetas. See M. Guimerá Peraza, *Maura y Galdós*, p. 142. The wages of workmen are taken from documents concerning the construction of Galdós's house in Santander, which documents are in the Casa-Museo Pérez Galdós, Las Palmas, Gran Canaria.

14. C. Bravo Villasante, "28 cartas de Galdós," *Cuadernos Hispanoamericanos*, nos. 250 - 52 (1970 - 1971), p. 11. The great book alluded to is *Gloria*.

15. We must remember that each volume was priced at two or three pesetas, practically a day's wages for the common man. Buying a book was a major outlay.

16. Letters from Ignacio Pérez Galdós to Benito speak of five debts assumed by the latter. Of these, figures are given for only two, but these represent an amount equal to half of the author's average annual income. These letters are in the Casa-Museo Pérez Galdós, Las Palmas.

17. The documents in the Casa-Museo Pérez Galdós include bills for more than 40,000 pesetas, many of which could not be paid for several years.

18. See Guimerá Peraza, *Maura y Galdós*, pp. 70 - 71; Clarín, *Galdós*, p. 338.

19. Documents in the Casa-Museo Pérez Galdós.

20. *The National Episodes*, forty-six in all, cannot be examined individually in a work of the present scope. They have recently been studied in detail in three books: H. Hinterhäuser, *Los "Episodios Nacionales" de Benito Pérez Galdós* (Madrid, 1963); Alfred Rodríguez, *An Introduction to the "Episodios Nacionales" of Galdós* (New York, 1967); and A. Regalado García, *Benito Pérez Galdós y la novela histórica española* (Madrid, 1966). Many articles have also dealt with the same subject.

21. *Gerona* is told by one of his friends.

22. B. P. G., *Memorias de un desmemoriado*, *O.C.*, VI, 1734, and the last paragraph of *La batalla de los Arapiles*, *O.C.*, I, 985.

23. *Episodios Nacionales* (Illustrated edition) Epilogue, p. iv; E. Varela Hervías, *Cartas de Pérez Galdós a Mesonero Romanos* (Madrid, 1943).

24. H. Levin, *The Gates of Horn* (New York: Oxford Univ. Press, 1963), p. 4.

Chapter Five

1. Galdós's review of Pereda's *Tipos y paisajes*, in *El Debate*, Jan. 26, 1872.

2. The book originally had a different ending, both in the serial form in the *Revista de España* and its first printing as an independent volume. Jacinto, whose plan to marry Rosario is thwarted by her insanity, conceives the idea of marrying Doña Perfecta, who, far from being saddened by Pepe Rey's death, is in better health and prettier than before. But when Jacinto enters a room where the women are cutting up a recently butchered hog, he slips and falls against his mother's knife, mortally wounding himself. See C. A. Jones, "Galdós's Second Thoughts on *Doña Perfecta*," *Modern Language Review* 54 (1959), 570.

3. R. G. Sánchez, "Doña Perfecta and the Histrionic Projection of a Character," *Revista de Estudios Hispánicos* 3 (1969), 175.

4. S. Gilman, "Las referencias clásicas de *Doña Perfecta*," *Nueva Revista de Filología Hispánica* 3 (194 - 99), 353; and R. Cardona, Introduction to *Doña Perfecta* (Dell Publishing Co., N.Y., 1965).

5. Clarín, *Galdós*, p. 27.

6. V. A. Chamberlin and Jack Weiner, "Galdós' *Doña Perfecta* and Turgenev's *Fathers and Sons*", *PMLA* 86 (1971), 19 - 24.

7. L. Alas (Clarín), *Galdós*, p. 28.

8. W. T. Pattison, "The Manuscript of *Gloria*," *Anales Galdosianos* 4 (1969), 55 - 61. I hope to publish the entire early versions soon.

9. W. T. Pattison, "The Genesis of *Gloria*", in *Galdós and the Creative Process*, esp. p. 20.

10. Berkowitz, *B. P. G. — Spanish Liberal Crusader*, p. 139 ff.; S. Ortega, *Cartas a Galdós*, pp. 49, 51 - 58, and 64 (letters from Pereda). Pereda also wrote a novel, *De tal palo*, clearly intended as an answer to *Gloria*.

11. W. T. Pattison, *Galdós and the Creative Process*, pp. 115 - 16.

12. Joaquín Casalduero, *Vida y obra de Galdós*, 2nd ed., p. 196 ff.

13. Pattison, *op. cit.*, pp. 120 - 31.

14. Juan López-Morillas, "Galdós y el krausismo," *Revista de Occidente*, no. 60 (March, 1968), esp. pp. 334 ff.

15. Alfred Rodríguez, "Algunos aspectos de la elaboración literaria de *La familia de León Roch*," *PMLA* 82 (1967), 121 - 27, sees a direct source of Galdós's novel in Jules Michelet, *Le Prêtre, la famille et la femme*. In Michelet's work the role of the confessor recalls Paoletti, but confessors are condemned in many anticlerical writings; specifically, there are significant resemblances to *León Roch's Family* in George Sand's *Mademoiselle La Quintinie*, 1863, a book which was in Galdós's library (6th ed., 1873). Raoul Narsy in the *Journal des Débats* (Jan. 16, 1920, pp. 107 - 08), finds a "striking analogy" between this book and *León Roch's Family*. In Sand's work the

confessor, Moreali, opposes the marriage of the Catholic Lucie to the freethinking Emile, just as he had opposed Lucie's mother's marriage to a freethinker. Both Emile and his father are examples of thoroughly ethical and tolerant men. They succeed in turning Lucie away from a narrow Catholicism and the convent. This denouement must have seemed to Galdós to be an impossibility in Spain.

Juan López-Morillas *(art. cit.)* sees *L. Roch's Family* as a realistic rectification of G. de Azcárate's *Minuta de un testamento,* in which a freethinker married to a Catholic wife succeeds in reconciling their opposed views and maintaining a happy marriage. As with Sand's work, such a solution is hardly possible in Galdós's opinion.

Chapter Six

1. The first two volumes of *León Roch's Family* had been published by Christmas, 1878, the third followed early in 1879. See E. Varela Hervías, *Cartas de P. Galdós a Mesonero Romanos,* p. 39 and S. Ortega, *Cartas a Galdós,* p. 30.

All six volumes of Zola in Galdós's library were printed in 1878. Given the extreme rapidity with which editions of Zola's works were exhausted, it is fair to say that the Spanish novelist must have bought them in the year they were published. The volume missing from his collection is *L'Assommoir* (1877), a work he must surely have read, as its *succès de scandale* was instrumental in bringing Zola to worldwide fame. Many works we know Galdós read are now missing from his library.

2. *O.C.,* II, 325.

3. For details see Pattison, "El amigo Manso and el amigo Galdós," in *Anales Galdosianos* 2 (1967) 135 - 53.

4. *El Imparcial,* May 9, 1881.

5. Luis Alfonso in *La Epoca,* Nov. 7, 1881.

6. M. B. Cossío, "Galdós y Giner," *La Lectura* 20, part I (1920), 254 - 58; W. H. Shoemaker, *Homenaje a Rodríguez Moñino* (Madrid: Castalia, 1966), II, 224.

7. For details see Pattison, *El naturalismo español,* pp. 126 - 30.

8. *El amigo Manso, O.C.,* IV, 1281.

9. See S. H. Eoff, *The Modern Spanish Novel,* pp. 120 - 22.

10. Eoff, *The Novels of Pérez Galdós,* p. 35.

11. Although Isidora's personality does not depend on environment there is evidence that Galdós studied it carefully in preparation for his work. Ortega Munilla *(El Imparcial,* Feb. 6, 1882) says that Galdós made several trips to Leganés to prepare the description of the insane asylum which opens the novel. He adds that the incidental characters are based on living people.

12. H. Levin, *The Gates of Horn,* p. 48.

13. "If you yearn to reach a difficult and craggy height, don't trust artificial wings. . . . Believe me, it will be best for you to take the stairs."

14. *O.C.*, IV, 973. Other examples of the same imaginative prefiguring of events are on pp. 1026, 1046, and 1049.

15. *Torquemada en la hoguera*, *O.C.*, V, 927 - 29.

16. For details on other models and on other matters concerning *Friend Manso* see Pattison, "El amigo Manso and el amigo Galdós," *Anales Galdosianos* 2 (1967), 135 - 53.

17. See Palacio Valdés in *Revista Europea* 11 (1878), 335 and 400; Clarín, *Galdós*, pp. 57 and 80.

18. For *Arte y Letras* see Pattison, *El naturalismo español*, p. 92; for *La Diana*, the first article of the first issue, reprinted in *El Imparcial*, Feb. 6, 1882.

19. *El Imparcial*, March 4, 1883.

20. On the banquet and attendant circumstances, see Berkowitz, *op. cit.*, pp. 164 - 72; Pattison, *op. cit.*, pp. 92 - 97.

21. Unlike Zola, who takes a discrete segment of reality as the subject matter of a book (a place: the mine, the department store, etc.; or a profession: the artist, the actress, etc.) neither Balzac nor Galdós compartmentalize their subject matter. Hence we feel that the technique of Balzac is more congenial to the Spaniard as is evident in this sequence of works.

22. Galdós, however, says he discovered Balzac in 1867. See above, p. 29.

23. *O.C.*, IV, 1305. A comparison with schools in Dickens's works shows striking similarities. In *Hard Times* M'Choakumchild and Gradgrind teach "hard facts" robbed of poetry. In *Dombey and Son* Dr. Blimber reduced "all the fancies" of poets to definitions and grammar, killing it as poetry. Like Dickens, Galdós also sees poetry in knowledge. When Dr. Moreno Rubio examines his patient the author comments, "This [examination] and the cantos of a beautiful poem came to be very similar things" (1409). Again, speaking of astronomy, Don Benito says "poetry gets into everything, even where it seems men are not looking for it, and thus . . . it appears in mathematics" (1296). H. Spencer, whom Galdós read and quotes in *Dr. Centeno*, also says that science is poetry (H. Spencer, *Education* . . . [New York: Appleton, 1914], p. 71).

24. Lazarillo de Tormes is the name character of the first picaresque novel (1554). Galdós saw a relationship between the picaresque novel and naturalism. See *Anales Galdosianos* 2 (1967), 150, n. 61.

25. "*Confiado*" has two meanings: "trusting, unsuspecting" and "presumptuous, self-confident, haughty." Both were true of Alejandro.

26. Spencer (*op. cit.*, chap. 1) condemns a classical education for boys, calling it an education "for ornamentation." Later (pp. 46 - 47 and 99) he declares that children should learn from *things*, not *books*.

27. Cf. Spencer's title: *Education, Intellectual, Moral and Physical*.

28. Galdós makes frequent use of Cervantes's phrase, even using it as the title of his last novel.

29. In two passages Galdós brings himself into the group of students living in the boarding house. He says, "Remember, reader, when you and I . . . lived in Doña Virginia's house" (p. 1358). (Doña Virginia owns the house where Alejandro and the others live.) Again he says that Alejandro asked all his friends "that *we* should take his pulse" (p. 1350).

30. The action of the novel takes place in 1867 and the first months of 1868. The revolution occurred in the following September.

31. See J. E. Varey, "Francisco Bringas: nuestro buen Thiers" in *Anales Galdosianos* 1 (1966), 63 - 64.

32. "La de Bringas," the title, implies a slight degree of scorn toward the protagonist, less than implied in our translation, but which would be absent from "Mrs. Bringas." Gerald Brenan translated the work under the title "The Spendthrifts," which avoids the difficulty but lacks relevance to the Spanish title.

33. Galdós visited this part of the palace, not shown to the public, in preparation for his novel. His description combines realism with the picturesqueness of *costumbrismo*.

34. Galdós's sister-in-law Magdalena had this same trouble with noises in her ears. R. Schmidt, *Cartas entre dos amigos del teatro,* pp. 42 and 47.

Galdós also had in his library a book which described some of the symptoms he attributes to the members of the Bueno de Guzmán family. This book (José Armangué y Tuset, *Estudios Clínicos de neuropatología* [Barcelona, 1884]) interested Don Benito especially because it dealt with migraine headaches, from which he suffered. He marked passages concerning this disorder, including one about disturbing noises in the ears (p. 212). On other pages he marked paragraphs concerning patients who imagine themselves suspended in the air (p. 211) or who are affected by stammering and loss of speech (p. 238).

35. Galdós undoubtedly knew Zola's writings, including his outline of the hereditary process first given in *La Fortune des Rougon* (1871), where he says that Pascal didn't seem to belong to the family and seemed to deny the laws of heredity. He explains that nature can produce an exception. Dr. Pascal and Camila have this in common.

36. Madame Warens, a philosophic and not sensual woman, suggested sexual relations to Rousseau, who was at that time still chaste, in order to keep him from vice. She gave him a week to think over her proposition, which seemed "most singular" to him. *Les Confessions,* Partie I, Livre V.

37. Clarín, *Galdós,* p. 135 ff.

38. In *El Imparcial,* May 11, 1885.

39. O. Lara y Pedraja, "Revista literaria," *Revista de España* 104 (1885), pp. 292 ff.

Chapter Seven

1. *El Imparcial,* April 18, 1887.
2. *El Imparcial,* April 13 and May 11, 1885.

3. *Ibid.*, Feb. 22, 1886.

4. Guayama, which had 59,827 inhabitants, gave Galdós 112 votes; 151 votes were "lost"! See M. Sánchez Ortiz, *Las primeras cámaras de la regencia* (Madrid, 1886), p. 541.

5. Oller in a letter of July 10, 1886. See W. H. Shoemaker, "Una amistad literaria . . . ," *Boletín de la Real Academia de Buenas Letras de Barcelona* 30 (1964), 278.

6. *Ibid.*, p. 279.

7. See his letter to Oller (W. H. Shoemaker, *op. cit.*, p. 282) and Clarín's letter to Galdós (S. Ortega, *Cartas a Galdós*, p. 243).

8. *Discursos leídos ante la Real Academia Española* (Madrid, 1897), pp. 87 -88.

9. V. A. Chamberlin and J. Weiner, "Galdós' *Doña Perfecta* and Turgenev's *Fathers and Sons*," *PMLA* 86 (1971), 19.

10. Shoemaker, *op. cit.*, p. 270.

11. E. M. Vogüé, in *Revue des Deux Mondes*, July 15, 1884 (vol. 64, p. 266), says "in a few days *War and Peace* will appear in the collection of foreign novels of the Hachette company." He gives the novel great praise (pp. 275 - 91).

12. Galdós, *Obras inéditas*, II, 206. Dated April 15, 1887.

13. *Obras inéditas*, VII, 36. Dated June 25, 1887.

14. In the French translation in three volumes (Paris, 1884).

15. E. Pardo Bazán, *La revolución y la novela en Rusia*, *Obras completas* (Madrid, Administración, 1907 ff.), vol. 33, pp. 429 - 30, and p. 439.

16. I cite the English translation by C. Garnett (New York: Random House, The Modern Library).

17. He also turned down pp. 865, 892, and 989 which deal with Karataev's story.

18. "Providence compelled all those men in striving for the attainment of their personal aims to combine in one immense result, of which no one individual man (not Napoleon, not Alexander, still less anyone taking practical part in the campaign) had the slightest inkling" (p. 637).

19. Compare Tolstoy's expressions of the same idea: ". . . all that he saw taking place that evening must inevitably be as it was" (p. 71); "All this had to be so and could not have been otherwise" (p. 193). Galdós had voiced the same thought as early as 1873; see *Anales Galdosianos* 2 (1967), 151, n. 73. Many of the ideas he found in *War and Peace* simply reinforced his own beliefs.

20. The same notion that historical law applies to both public and private life occurs in another passage: "She [Doña Lupe] thought with remarkable insight that when in the private, just as in the public, order a powerful revolutionary impulse is begun . . . it is madness to oppose it" (202a). And on a third page, referring to Fortunata's return to Maxi: "It was one of those things which happen, without anyone's being able to determine how they come to pass, fatal happenings in the history of a family like similar events in

the history of nations . . . [without] anyone's seeing the hidden mechanism which brings them on" (362b).

21. See Vera Colin, "A Note on Tolstoy and Galdós," in *Anales Galdosianos* 2 (1967), 155 - 68; and "Tolstoy and *Angel Guerra*" in *Galdós Studies* (London, 1970), pp. 115 - 35.

22. On Dec. 8, 1884, not long before the period in which Galdós gathered materials for *Fortunata* . . . (see p. 136), he wrote to Oller praising his novel *La papalona*. "As for the subject," he says, "there are probably few more pathetic. The seduction and sacrifice of the unfortunate working girl of our times is one of the most beautiful that the novelist can use" (Shoemaker, *op. cit.*, p. 266). Oller's heroine, Toneta, a seamstress seduced and abandoned by a student, seeks and gets help from a society woman with whom she leaves her child when her own milk is insufficient and the baby is starving. After the death of the rich lady's child, Toneta's baby is dressed in the dead boy's clothes and passed off as the society woman's for a while. Like Fortunata, Toneta dies. These are vague similarities; still the suggestion of Galdós's Fortunata may lie in Oller's Toneta.

23. The selling of children was not uncommon, as Galdós's friend Tolosa Latour, a great benefactor of children, reveals in an article in *La Epoca*, Aug. 11, 1884. He answers another article by V. Colorado (*ibid.*, June 23, 1884), who relates a specific incident of a sale in which he took part.

24. This theme was discerned soon after the publication of the book. See the words of Oller to Galdós in a letter of Nov. 28, 1887 (Shoemaker, *op. cit.*, p. 285): "No one here [in Spain] has set forth so clearly the brutal, unending battle, the cause of our wretchedness, which nature wages against the conventionalities of civilization."

25. Perhaps Galdós chose to name his creature Fortunata because of this subjection to Fate (Latin, *Fortuna*, the goddess of chance and fate, but also of fertility. Both aspects apply to Galdós's heroine).

26. We are reminded of Goethe's *Elective Affinities*, which Galdós possessed in the French translation by Camille Selden (Paris, 1872). (Among Maxi's readings Don Benito names Goethe's *Werther* and *Faust*, in French translation [179a], but not the *Elective Affinities*.)

Goethe's idea is that human attractions are just like chemical combinations. If two solutions containing compounds AB and XY are mixed the elements may rearrange themselves so that AY will precipitate as a solid leaving the compound BX in solution. He applies this highly deterministic notion to the married couple of his novel, making each one of them gravitate irresistibly to another person. Fortunata's fascination with Mauricia as well as her unswerving love for the worthless Juanito are reminiscent of the unexplained laws of nature basic to Goethe's thought. In Galdós's copy of Heine, *Reisebilder — Tableaux de voyage* (Paris, 1863) he marked a passage (p. 107) where Heine talks of the laws of nature as developed by Goethe in *Les Affinités électives*.

27. A few months later when Fortunata visits Don Evaristo for the last

time she finds him senile. Galdós comments on their friendship, calling Evaristo her "great and useful friend, the best man whom she had dealt with in her life and surely also the most practical, the wisest, and the one who gave the best advice" (476a). Are we to assume then that Feijoo's ideas on natural and socialized love are those of the author himself? Yet when Juanito excuses his conduct saying that social custom permits infidelities not condoned by absolute morality — essentially the heart of Don Evaristo's philosophy — Galdós declares that "it was all conventionalism and ingenious phrases in that man" (64a). Evidently the author does not equate antisocial freedom in love with promiscuity.

28. Doña Guillermina is clearly modeled on a real-life woman, Ernestina Villena, about whom Galdós wrote an article, collected in *Obras inéditas*, VII, 7 - 17. J. L. Brooks, "The Character of Doña Guillermina Pacheco," *Bulletin of Hispanic Studies* 38 (1961), 86 - 94, points out that this character, whom Galdós often calls a saint, is in reality limited by restrictions of class and religion. See also Lucille V. Braun, "Galdós' Recreation of Ernestina de Villena as Guillermina Pacheco," *Hispanic Review* 38 (1970), 32 - 55.

29. See in n. 21 the two articles of Vera Colin cited above.

30. Translated by C. Garnett, Modern Library, pp. 947 - 50.

31. Juanito follows a trend popular at the time, imitating the customs and language of the low quarters. See Ortega Munilla in *El Imparcial*, June 19, 1882, who says that idle young men are bringing a plague of *flamenquismo* into customs and speech of the upper classes.

32. Estupiñá was a real man, José Luengo by name. See O.C., VI, 1737b.

33. The decline of the trade in Spanish shawls (29 - 30) is reminiscent of the deterioration of old-fashioned shops, such as *Au viel Elbeuf* (in Zola, *Au bonheur des dames*, pp. 6, 16, 21, and 28), a business overwhelmed by the new department store because it does not abandon traditional ways.

34. Don Benito speaks of careful investigation to gather materials for the novel, O.C., VI, 1737b, and in the preface to *Misericordia* (W. H. Shoemaker, *Los prólogos de Galdós*, p. 109).

35. An example: the child Jacinta wants to adopt, believing it to be Juanito's son, is brought home on the Día de los Inocentes (the Spanish equivalent to April Fools' Day).

36. See the bibliographies of H. C. Woodbridge and T. A. Sackett in the Selected Bibliography.

37. Ricardo Gullón, "Estructura y diseño en *Fortunata y Jacinta*" in *Papeles de Son Armadans* 48 (1968), 223 - 315.

38. J. Casalduero, "*Ana Karenina y Realidad*," *Bulletin Hispanique* 39 (1937), 394.

39. O.C., V, 297a and 304. In these passages the time of the action is 1874 (*ibid.*, 298a), before the Restoration in the person of Alfonso XII (304a and b). But in *Miau* Villamil is at the same stage of his life, that is, lacking two months service for retirement, and the date is 1878 (Ed. By R. Gullón, p. 352). The tomb of Rameses II was found in 1881, so Villamil's nickname is

opportune at the time *Miau* was written, but not so at the action time of the novel.

40. Page 352 in the edition of Ricardo Gullón, Ediciones de la Universidad de Puerto Rico, Revista de Occidente (Madrid, 1957). Hereafter references to this edition will be inserted parenthetically in the text.

41. Casalduero, *op. cit.*, 394.

42. Gullón, *op. cit.*, 295 - 302.

43. See some examples cited by Robert J. Weber, *The Miau Manuscript . . . ,* pp. 1 - 6. Ortega Munilla praises Eusebio Blasco's *Busilis*, a novel dealing with bureaucracy *(El Imparcial,* Oct. 25, 1880).

Chapter Eight

1. Clarín, *Galdós*, p. 219, blames Don Benito for his monologues, calling them the words of the author put in the mouths of his characters. Elsewhere he states that the dramatic form is a mistake *(ibid.,* p. 200).

2. Who was already named in *Lo prohibido, O.C.,* IV, 1768.

3. As first stated by José Yxart, *El arte escénico en España,* I, 316.

4. *La incógnita* (Buenos Aires: Editorial Losada, 1944), p. 175. Subsequent page references in the text are to this edition.

5. *Realidad* (Buenos Aires: Editorial Losada, 1944), p. 251. Page references in the text are to this edition.

6. *Anna Karenina,* part IV, chapters 17 and 18.

7. *Ibid.,* chapters 19 and 21. George Portnoff, *La literatura rusa en España,* pp. 132 - 71, argues for this source. Shirley Fite, "The Literary Origins of *Realidad,*" *Dissertation Abstracts* 19 (1959), 2088, agrees with Portnoff, but Casalduero, "*Ana Karenina y Realidad,*" *Bulletin Hispanique* 39 (1937), 375 - 96, contradicts Portnoff's belief. Tolstoy's novel is not in Galdós's library (as now preserved), but it was available in translations in both French (1885) and Spanish (1888).

8. Articles reprinted in *Obras inéditas,* VII, 87 - 144.

9. S. Fite, *op. cit.*

10. See Pardo Bazán, *Nuevo Teatro Crítico,* April, 1892, p. 19 ff.

11. As was his custom, Galdós put the date of composition at the end of the manuscripts of *The Unknown* (Nov. 1888 - Feb. 1889) and *Reality* (July, 1889). But the two books were not published at these times. See *El Imparcial,* Oct. 7, 1889.

12. The *Revue Indepéndante* printed nineteen pages of *The Doll's House* (French translation by Prozor) in Oct., 1888, and all of *Ghosts* in Jan., 1889. In this latter year the full translations of both plays were published by Albert Savine (before August, when articles by Jules Lemaître based on them appeared in the *Journal des Débats).* Since Savine had written the preface to the French translation of *Doña Perfecta* (1885) and translated Pardo Bazán's *Cuestión palpitante* (1886), there is a good chance that he sent copies of the Ibsen translations to these Spaniards. In Galdós's library, however, we find only the second edition, 1892.

13. *La incógnita*, pp. 55 - 58. Cf. Berkowitz, *B. P. G. — Spanish Liberal Crusader*, p. 198.

14. *La incógnita*, p. 11. For Galdós, see above, p. 13.

15. *Ibid.*, pp. 61 and 121.

16. *Ibid.*, pp. 101 and 115 - 16. Intuition is likened to poetry which precedes factual knowledge, an idea already expressed in *Fortunata . . .*, *O.C.*, V, 490.

17. Oller, *Memòries literàries*, p. 116; Shoemaker, *Una amistad literaria*, p. 287.

18. Galdós wrote an account of this trip: *O.C.*, VI, 1675 - 85.

19. See Berkowitz, *B. P. G. — Spanish Liberal Crusader*, pp. 186 - 88.

20. For Galdós's own account, see *O.C.*, VI, 1685, 1719.

21. See Galdós, "La casa de Shakespeare", *O.C.*, VI, 1479 - 86.

22. See Pattison, "Two Women in the Life of Galdós," in *Anales Galdosianos*, 8 (1973), pp. 23 - 31.

23. Her letter urging him to publish in *La España Moderna* is in the Casa-Museo Pérez Galdós, dated Dec. 7, 1888.

24. For details of Galdós's relation with Lorenza, see article cited in n. 22.

25. See F. L. Lucas, *Literature and Psychology* (Ann Arbor: Univ. of Michigan Press, 1962), p. 92: "Yet another variety of fatal reversion to the situations of childhood is what one may call "Petrarchan passion" — where the lover wishes only to love the unattainable, as a moth, a star — . . . without ever making an effort to approach and win 'la princesse lointaine', in whom the parent unattainably loved in childhood is incarnate once more."

26. Francisco Ruiz Ramón, *Tres personajes galdosianos* (Madrid: Revista de Occidente, 1964), pp. 50 - 52.

27. Guerra's ideas show a strong similarity to those of Tolstoy, as shown especially in *My Religion*. See V. Colin, "Tolstoy and *A. Guerra*," in *Galdós Studies*, ed. J. E. Varey (London, 1970).

28. See G. Marañón, "Galdós en Toledo" in *Elogio y nostalgia de Toledo*, esp. p. 170.

29. Trino Peraza de Ayala, *La psiquiatría española en el siglo XIX* (Madrid: Consejo Superior de Investigaciones Científicas, 1947), tells us that psychiatry was practically nonexistent in nineteenth-century Spain. But he mentions three doctors, friends of Galdós, interested in insanity: Pedro Mata (p. 89 ff.), Esquerdo (pp. 129 - 31), and Tolosa Latour (pp. 145 - 46). The last named, an intimate of Don Benito, published *La locura en la infancia* (1881), in which he says parents are often the cause of children's insanity.

30. *La loca de la casa* is literally "the mad woman of the house" and it is a phrase often used as synonymous with "imagination." The heroine of the work is in fact an imaginative, intuitive, even mystic person.

31. Berkowitz, *B. P. G. — Spanish Liberal Crusader*, p. 314.

32. *Tristana* (Buenos Aires: Losada, 1943), pp. 25, 61, 68, 73, 81, 90, 96, and 112. Henceforth page references in the text will be given to this edition.

33. See Pattison, *Emilia Pardo Bazán* (New York: Twayne Publishers, 1971), p. 66.

34. *O.C.*, VI, 722b.

35. Robert J. Weber, "Galdós' Preliminary Sketches for *Torquemada y San Pedro*," *Bul. of Hispanic Studies* 44 (1967), 16 - 27.

36. Auguste Comte equated Humanity with God. See Pattison, *Galdós and the Creative Process*, p. 120, n. 20.

37. See Douglas Rogers, "Lenguaje y personaje en Galdós: un estudio de Torquemada," *Cuadernos Hispanoamericanos*, no. 206 (Feb., 1967), pp. 243 - 73.

Chapter Nine

1. Four articles on Nazarín as a Christ-figure by F. P. Bowman, C. Morón Arroyo, A. A. Parker, and R. H. Russell appear in *Anales Galdosianos* 2 (1967). They were reprinted in a supplementary volume in 1967.

2. A nickname contracted from Ana de Ara, says Galdós *(O.C.*, V, 1694a). He possibly also had the Basque word for "lady," *andara*, in mind, in keeping with his ironical view of reality. He was interested in the Basque language although not proficient in it. He makes Nazarín call Andara "señora" at times, *v.g. ibid.*, 1692a.

3. For details, see Pattison, "Verdaguer y Nazarín," *Cuadernos Hispanoamericanos*, nos. 250 - 52 (Oct., 1970 - Jan., 1971), 537 - 45.

4. Of course *"Halma"* is identical to *"alma"* ("soul") in pronunciation.

5. It is also Tolstoy's belief that aid should be offered without questioning the worthiness of the receiver.

6. Beggars are no longer so visible in Spain, whereas formerly they were numerous, especially around the doors of churches.

7. Related to Jesús Delgado (in *Dr. Centeno*) and, like Jesús, mentally disturbed.

8. Saint Rita, 1377 - 1447, was canonized May 24, 1900. Perhaps discussion of her canonization took place as early as 1897, while Galdós was preparing *Compassion*. Her attribute as the "advocate of desperate cases" makes Benina's comparison to her significant.

9. *Misericordia* (Paris: Thomas and Sons, n.d.), *Prefacio del autor*, pp. 5 - 9.

10. Clarín, *Galdós*, p. 301.

11. *Ibid.*, p. 298.

12. *Ibid.*, p. 294.

Chapter Ten

1. Shoemaker, article cited in chap. 7, n. 5, p. 288.

2. R. Schmidt, *Cartas entre dos amigos del teatro: M. Tolosa Latour y B. Pérez Galdós*, pp. 73, 90, 95.

3. See T. Alvarez Angulo, *Memorias de un hombre sin importancia* (Madrid: Aguilar, 1962), p. 548. On the other hand, the new generation of

young authors called Galdós's work "not just decadent, but something even worse; his last book is almost always [called] an insupportable bore." F. Urrecha in *El Imparcial*, Jan. 2, 1893.

4. Mario Verdaguer, *Medio siglo de la vida barcelonesa*, p. 48.

5. S. de la Nuez y J. Schraibman, *Cartas del archivo de Galdós*, p. 90.

6. Berkowitz, *B. P. G. — Spanish Liberal Crusader*, pp. 417 and 420 - 30.

7. In newspaper clippings in the Casa-Museo Pérez Galdós, Galdós states that Romero was supposed to give him 1,000 pesetas a month but paid only instalments of 100 or 200 pesetas and that reluctantly. Romero says Galdós attributed his poverty to his "vipers, hangmen, and sharpers, as he piously called his creditors" but that he used the money given him "in order to have the wherewithal to pay his caprices — carriages, Havana cigars, and other details which I resist naming." The latter phrase has been taken by some to mean sordid love affairs. Romero was answered indignantly by Federico García Sánchiz. "Do you know what causes Galdós's constant economic pinch? Sponging, sponging by innumerable parasites, attacks which the childish old man could never resist."

8. Casa-Museo Pérez Galdós, Carpeta 16, Legajo 1. Dated only Dec. 9. Another letter signed by Ferrer contains a threat to kill Galdós. *Ibid.*, Carpeta 2, Legajo 70.

9. Collected in *Nuestro Teatro, Obras inéditas*, V.

10. Quoted by Berkowitz, *B. P. G. — Spanish Liberal Crusader*, p. 243. Ortega Munilla (in *El Imparcial*, April 4 and 18, 1892) thinks Galdós was tempted to adapt *Reality* to the stage because novels paid so poorly.

11. See my article cited in chap. 8, n. 22; and Berkowitz, *op. cit.*, p. 263 and 283 - 84.

12. Galdós complains of critical indifference to all novels in the prologue of *The Condemned (O.C.,* VI, 726a).

13. *Nuestro Teatro*, p. 162, and *O.C.*, VI, 725a and 728a.

14. Probably Galdós was thinking of his friend Tolosa Latour's asylum at Chipiona, to which Don Benito made contributions.

15. Galdós, *Memorias de un desmemoriado, O.C.,* VI, 1769b.

16. The same romantic situation is parodied in Bretón de los Herreros's *Muérete y verás*, which may have inspired Galdós's scene.

17. Galdós models Marcela on Cervantes's character of the same name. See *Don Quixote*, part I, chaps. 12 - 14.

18. Halconero, the farmer, has Galdós's respect as producer of real wealth and hence a benefactor of the nation.

19. See Hinterhäuser, *Los Episodios Nacionales*, p. 74.

20. The first peasant uprising took place at Loja in 1861 and is depicted by Galdós in the Episode *La vuelta del mundo en la Numancia* (The Circumnavigation of the World in the Numancia), *O.C.*, III, 442 ff. In Barcelona the textile workers struck for the first time in 1854. The conditions which provoked these popular rebellions are a principal factor in Galdós's protest against the politicosocial situation.

21. *O.C.*, III, 557 and 562 - 63.

22. Titus Livius, the Roman historian, whose name is deformed to *liviano*, "light, fickle; lewd."

23. Some biographers see these sexual encounters as a reflection of Galdós's own life. He certainly disapproves of Tito and uses his affairs as a biting commentary of the low morals of the times.

24. M. Enguídanos, "Mariclío, musa galdosiana," *Papeles de Son Armandans* 43 (1961), 235 - 49.

25. J. Casalduero, *Vida y obra de Galdós*, 2nd ed., p. 165.

26. Don Juan de Urríes and Tito (both characters of the Fifth Series) are cheapened avatars of Don Juan. Juan Ruiz Hondón (in *Carlos VI en la Rápita*) is modeled on the medieval poet Juan Ruiz. Wifredo Romarate *(España sin rey)* is a Quixote.

27. A good example is the Marqués de Abdalá (in *Love and Learning* [*O.C.* VI, 1132b and 1150a]), who is identical to Evaristo Feijoo *(Fortunata . . .)*. In the same play Dr. Bruno is reminiscent of León Roch. Obdulia of the Fifth Series of *National Episodes* is so like the Obdulia of *Misericordia* that it "suggests an inadvertent duplication by Galdós" (A. Rodríguez, *Introduction to the "Episodios Nacionales,"* p. 187).

28. M. Guimerá Peraza, *Maura y Galdós*, pp. 124 and 69.

29. Berkowitz, *B. P. G. — Spanish Liberal Crusader*, p. 345.

30. Galdós received accounts on the earnings of his plays (almost entirely from *Electra*) during the trimester April through June, 1901, from D. Hidalgo of the *Administración Lírico-Dramática, Hijos de E. Hidalgo*. The letter enclosing the accounts is dated Aug. 19, 1901. Of the 16,515 pesetas earned, Galdós has received all but 65 pesetas. At this same time he was not able to liquidate a loan from Encarnación Gómez, taken in Oct., 1898, and continuing to Jan., 1904, originally at 24 percent, later reduced to 12 percent after Galdós recommended her son as an actor. (Documents in the Casa-Museo Pérez Galdós.)

31. Letter of Manuel Blasco Vicat, June 3, 1913, on stationery of *El Crédito de la Propiedad Intelectual* (Casa-Museo Pérez Galdós, Carpeta 37, Legajo 23). In the month of April of the same year, his plays earned him only 462 pesetas, according to the account rendered by the Sociedad de Autores Españoles.

32. Libro auxiliar: cuenta de gastos. Año 1919. Nov. and Dec. (In Casa-Museo Pérez Galdós).

33. P. Beltrán de Heredia, "España en la muerte de Galdós," *Anales Galdosianos*, V, 89.

34. Berkowitz, *op. cit.*, p. 409.

35. Pattison, "Two Women in the Life of Galdós," *Anales Galdosianos* 8 (1973), 29.

36. Berkowitz, *op. cit.*, 410 and 418.

37. P. Beltrán de Heredia, *op. cit.*, p. 92.

38. *Ibid.*, p. 100. There are excellent photographs of the elderly author and his funeral in this article.

Selected Bibliography

PRIMARY SOURCES

The commonly used "official" edition of Galdós's works is that published by Aguilar, Madrid: 1941, six volumes, frequently reprinted, with introduction and catalogues of characters by F. C. Sainz de Robles. It leaves much to be desired, especially because the pagination of the various printings is not uniform. Hence page citations are often difficult to run down.

In the present work the abbreviation *O. C.* refers to the Aguilar publication, of which we used the volumes of the following reprintings: I (1945), II (1944), III (1945), IV (1949), V (1950), and VI (1942). The indexes of Galdós's characters, at the end of volumes III and VI, lose much of their usefulness owing to the changed pagination of the various printings.

The dates given below are those Galdós ascribed to the time of composition of the works and not necessarily the dates of publication.

1. Novels of the First Period:
La fontana de oro. 1867-68.
La sombra. 1867 (?).
El audaz. 1871.
Doña Perfecta. 1876.

Gloria. 2 vols., 1876-77.
Marianela. 1878.
La familia de León Roch. 3 vols., 1878-79.

2. Contemporary Spanish Novels:
La desheredada. 1881.
El amigo Manso. 1882.
El doctor Centeno. 2 vols., 1883.
Tormento. 1884.
La de Bringas. 1884.
Lo prohibido. 2 vols., 1884-85.
Fortunata y Jacinta. 4 vols., 1886-87.
Miau. 1888.
La incógnita. 1888-89.
Torquemada en la hoguera. 1889.
Realidad. 1889.
Angel Guerra. 3 vols., 1890-91.

Tristana. 1892.
La loca de la casa. 1892.
Torquemada en la Cruz. 1893.
Torquemada en el purgatorio. 1894.
Torquemada y San Pedro. 1895.
Nazarín. 1895.
Halma. 1895.
Misericordia. 1897.
El abuelo. 1897.
Casandra. 1905.
El caballero encantado. 1909.
La razón de la sinrazón. 1915.

3. *National Episodes:*

First Series

Trafalgar. 1873.   *Zaragoza.* 1874.
La corte de Carlos IV. 1873.   *Gerona.* 1874.
El 19 de marzo y el 2 de mayo. 1873.   *Cádiz.* 1874.
Bailén. 1873.   *Juan Martín el Empecinado.* 1874.
Napoleón en Chamartín. 1874.   *La batalla de los Arapiles.* 1875.

Second Series

El equipaje del Rey José. 1875.   *El terror de 1824.* 1877.
Memorias de un cortesano. 1875.   *Un voluntario realista.* 1878.
La segunda casaca. 1876.   *Los apostólicos.* 1879.
El Grande Oriente. 1876.   *Un faccioso más y algunos frailes
El 7 de julio. 1876.   menos.* 1879.
Los cien mil hijos de San Luis. 1877.

Third Series

Zumalacárregui. 1898   *La estafeta romántica.* 1899.
Mendizábal. 1898.   *Vergara.* 1899.
De Oñate a la Granja. 1898.   *Montes de Oca.* 1900.
Luchana. 1899.   *Los ayacuchos.* 1900.
La campaña del Maestrazgo. 1899.   *Bodas reales.* 1900.

Fourth Series

Las tormentas del 48. 1902.   *Carlos VI en la Rápita.* 1905.
Narváez. 1902.   *La vuelta al mundo en la
Los duendes de la camarilla. 1903.   Numancia.* 1906.
La revolución de julio. 1903-04.   *Prim.* 1906.
O'Donnell. 1904.   *La de los tristes destinos.* 1907.
Aita Tettauen. 1904-05.

Final Series

España sin rey. 1907-08.   *La primera república.* 1911.
España trágica. 1909.   *De Cartago a Sagunto.* 1911.
Amadeo I. 1910.   *Cánovas.* 1912.

4. Drama:

Realidad. 1892.   *El abuelo.* 1904.
La loca de la casa. 1893.   *Bárbara.* 1905.
Gerona. 1893.   *Amor y ciencia.* 1905.
La de San Quintín. 1894.   *Pedro Minio.* 1908.
Los condenados. 1894.   *Casandra.* 1910.
Voluntad. 1895.   *Celia en los infiernos.* 1913.
Doña Perfecta. 1896.   *Alceste.* 1914.
La fiera. 1896.   *Sor Simona.* 1915.
Electra. 1901.   *El tacaño Salomón.* 1916.
Alma y vida. 1902.   *Santa Juana de Castilla.* 1918.
Mariucha. 1903.

5. Miscellaneous Works:
"Observaciones sobre la novela côntemporánea en España." *Revista de España* 15 (1870), 162-72.

"Discursos académicos." 1897.
"Memoranda." 1906.

6. Works Published Posthumously:
Fisonomías sociales.
Arte y crítica.
Política española. 2 vols.
Nuestro teatro.
Cronicón. 2 vols.

Toledo.
Viajes y fantasías.
Memorias.
Crónica de Madrid.

SECONDARY SOURCES

In a work of this scope it has been necessary to limit strictly the number of sources cited. The author begs the indulgence of those excluded. For additional bibliography see the works of Hernández Suárez, Sackett, and Woodbridge listed below.

ALAS, LEOPOLDO (CLARÍN). *Benito Pérez Galdós.* Madrid: 1889. 2nd ed., 1912.

ANTÓN DEL OLMET, LUIS and ARTURO GARCÍA CARRAFFA. *Los grandes españoles: Galdós.* Madrid: Alrededor del mundo, 1912.

ARMAS AYALA, ALFONSO. "Galdós y sus cartas." *Papeles de Son Armadans* 40 (Jan. - Mar., 1966), 9 - 36.

BERKOWITZ, H. CHONON. *Benito Pérez Galdós: Spanish Liberal Crusader.* Madison: University of Wisconsin Press, 1948.

———. *La biblioteca de Benito Pérez Galdós.* Las Palmas: El Museo Canario, 1951.

———. "Galdós' Literary Apprenticeship." *Hispanic Review* 3 (1935), 1 - 22.

BLANQUAT, JOSETTE. "Au temps d'*Electra*." *Bulletin Hispanique*, 68 (1966), 253 - 308.

BROOKS, J. L. "The Character of Doña Guillermina Pacheco in Galdós' novel *Fortunata y Jacinta*." *Bulletin of Hispanic Studies* 38 (1961), 86 - 94.

BROWN, DONALD F. "More Light on the Mother of Galdós." *Hispania* 39 (1956), 403 - 08.

CASALDUERO, JOAQUÍN. *Vida y obra de Galdós.* 2nd ed. Madrid: Gredos, 1951.

———. "*Ana Karenina y Realidad*." *Bulletin Hispanique* 39 (1937), 375 - 96.

CLAVERÍA, CARLOS. "Sobre la veta fantástica en la obra de Galdós." *Atlante* (London), 1 (1953), 78 - 86, 136 - 43.

COLIN, VERA. "A Note on Tolstoy and Galdós." *Anales Galdosianos* 2 (1967), 155 - 68.

CORREA, GUSTAVO. *El simbolismo religioso en las novelas de Pérez Galdós.* Madrid: Gredos, 1962.

COSSÍO, JOSÉ MARÍA DE. *Rutas literarias de la montaña.* Santander, 1960.

COSSÍO, MANUEL B. "Galdós y Giner. Una carta de Galdós." *La Lectura* 20, no. 1 (March, 1920), 254 - 58.

EOFF, SHERMAN HINKLE. *The Modern Spanish Novel.* New York: New York University Press, 1961.

————. *The Novels of Pérez Galdós: The Concept of Life as Dynamic Process.* St. Louis: Washington University Studies, 1954.

GREGERSEN, HALFDAN. *Ibsen and Spain: A Study in Comparative Drama.* Cambridge: Harvard Press, 1936.

GULLÓN, RICARDO. *Galdós, novelista moderno.* Madrid: Taurus, 1960.

————. *Técnicas de Galdós.* Madrid: Taurus, 1970.

HERNÁNDEZ SUÁREZ, MANUEL. "Bibliografía." *Anales Galdosianos* 3 (1968), 4 (1969), 6 (1971), and 7 (1972). His bibliography in a separate volume is announced for publication in 1974.

HINTERHÄUSER, HANS. *Los 'Episodios nacionales' de Benito Pérez Galdós.* Madrid: Gredos, 1963.

JOBIT, PIERRE. *Les Éducateurs de l'Espagne Contemporaine,* vol. I, Les Krausistas. Paris: Bibliothèque de l'École des Hautes Études Hispaniques, 1936.

JONES, C. A. "Galdós's Second Thoughts on *Doña Perfecta.*" *Modern Language Review* 54 (1959), 570 - 73.

LÓPEZ-MORILLAS, JUAN. "Historia y novela en el Galdós primerizo: en torno a *La Fontana de Oro.*" *Revista Hispánica Moderna* 31, nos. 1-4 (Jan. - Oct., 1965), 273 - 84.

————. *El krausismo español.* México: Fondo de Cultura Económica, 1956.

MARAÑON, GREGORIO DE, *Eloqio y nostalqia ole Toledo.* Madrid: Espasa-Calpe, 1958.

————. *Efemérides y comentarios.* Madrid: 1955.

————. "Galdós íntimo." *La Lectura,* vol. 1 (1920), 64 - 88.

MENÉNDEZ y PELAYO, MARCELINO, Benito Pérez Galdós y José María de Pereda. *Discursos leídos ante la Real Academia Española.* Madrid: 1897.

MONTESINOS, JOSÉ F. *Galdós: Estudios sobre la novela española del siglo XIX.* 3 vols. Madrid: Castalia, 1968 - 72.

NUEZ, SEBASTIÁN DE LA y SCHRAIBMAN, JOSÉ. *Cartas del archivo de Galdós.* Madrid: Taurus, 1967.

————"Unamuno y Galdós en sus cartas." *Ínsula* 19, nos. 216 - 17 (1964),29.

OBAID, ANTONIO. "Galdós y Cervantes." *Hispania* 41 (1958), 269 - 73.

ORTEGA, SOLEDAD. *Cartas a Galdós.* Madrid: Revista de Occidente, 1965.

PATTISON, WALTER T. *Benito Pérez Galdós and the Creative Process.* Minneapolis: University of Minnesota Press, 1954.

————. *El naturalismo español.* Madrid: Gredos, 1965.

————. "Nazarín y Verdaguer." *Cuadernos Hispanoamericanos,* no. 250 - 2 (1970 - 71), 537 - 45.

PÉREZ VIDAL, JOSÉ. *Galdós en Canarias (1843 - 1862)*. Las Palmas: 1952.

PORTNOFF, G. *La literatura rusa en España*. New York: Instituto de las Españas, 1932.

REGALADO GARCÍA, ANTONIO. *Benito Pérez Galdós y la novela histórica española: 1868 - 1912*. Madrid: Ínsula, 1966.

RODRÍGUEZ, ALFRED. *An Introduction to the 'Episodios nacionales' of Galdós*. New York: Las Américas, 1967.

————. "Algunos aspectos de la elaboración literaria de *La familia de León Roch*." *PMLA* 72 (1967). 121 - 27.

RUIZ RAMÓN, FRANCISCO. *Tres personajes galdosianos*. Madrid: Revista de Occidente, 1964

SACKETT, THEODORE A. *Pérez Galdós: An Annotated Bibliography*. Albuquerque: University of New Mexico Press, 1968.

SCHMIDT, RUTH. *Cartas entre dos amigos del teatro: Manuel Tolosa Latour y Benito Pérez Galdós*. Las Palmas: Ediciones del Excmo. Cabildo de Gran Canaria, 1969.

SCHRAIBMAN, JOSEPH. *Dreams in the Novels of Galdós*. New York: Hispanic Institute, 1960.

————. "Galdós, colaborador de *El Omnibus*." *Anuario de Estudios Atlánticos* (Madrid-Las Palmas) 9 (1963), 289 - 334

SHOEMAKER, W. H. *Los artículos de Galdós en "La Nación."* Madrid: Insula, 1972.

————. *Los prólogos de Galdós*. Mexico: University of Illinois Press, Ediciones de Andrea, 1962.

————. "Una amistad literaria: La correspondencia epistolar entre Galdós y Narciso Oller." *Boletín de la Real Academia de Buenas Letras de Barcelona* 30 (1963 - 64), 247 - 306.

UGARTE, M. *Visiones de España*. Valencia: Sempere, 1904.

VARELA HERVÍAS, Eulogio. *Cartas de Pérez Galdós a Mesonero Romanos*. Madrid: Artes gráficas municipales, 1943.

VAREY, J. E. "Francisco Bringas: nuestro buen Thiers." *Anales Galdosianos* (1966), 63 - 69.

VERDAGUER, MARIO. *Medio siglo de vida íntima barcelonesa*. Barcelona: Barna, 1957.

WEBER, ROBERT J. *The 'Miau' Manuscript of Pérez Galdós: A Critical Study*. Berkeley and Los Angeles: University of California Press, 1964.

————. "Galdós' Preliminary Sketches for *Torquemada y San Pedro*." *Bulletin of Hispanic Studies*. 44 (1967), 16 - 27.

WOODBRIDGE, HENSLEY C. "Benito Pérez Galdós: A Selected Annotated Bibliography." *Hispania* 53 (1970), 899 - 971.

YXART, JOSÉ. *El arte escénico en España*. Barcelona: La Vanguardia, 1894. 2 vols.

ZULUETA, CARMEN. *Navarro Ledesma: el hombre y su tiempo*. Madrid and Barcelona: Alfaguara, 1968.

Index

863.5
P438